MW00445696

WORKBOOK
Genesis Curriculum
The Book of Genesis

2019 Edition

This workbook belongs to

Riley

Copyright © 2019 Lee Giles
All Rights Reserved
ISBN : 9781533523754

Hebrew verse images used with permission from
http://www.mechon-mamre.org/p/pt/pt0101.htm.

Hebrew letter tracing images are used with permission from Hebrew4Christians.
http://www.hebrew4christians.com/
They have many pages of tracing and copywork available on their site.

Thank you to PuzzleFast for allowing use of their puzzles in our workbook.

If you don't want to cut your workbook, those activity pages
can be printed from our site, genesiscurriculum.com.
Find them through the Online Support page.

Table of Contents:

Writing/Editing.................1
Writing Sentences............5
Spelling Review..............29
Grammar Review............65
Vocabulary Review.........75
Science Review..............91
Social Studies Review...117
Hebrew Writing............143
Appendix......................203
Day number index is in the appendix.

Paragraph Writing

Introduction (What's the main idea?)

_____

_____

_____

Detail 1 _____

_____

_____

Detail 2 _____

_____

_____

Detail 3 _____

_____

_____

Conclusion (What's the point?)

_____

_____

_____

Essay Writing Outline (The Plan)

The intro, the three main ideas, and the conclusion will each become a paragraph.

Introduction: What's the main idea?

Get their attention (first sentence): _____

_____

Thesis statement (last sentence): _____

_____

Body: Prove your idea. Give the details that support your thesis.

Main idea 1:_____

_____

Main idea 2:_____

_____

Main idea 3:_____

_____

Conclusion: What's the point?

Restate your thesis in a different way (first sentence): _____

_____

Wrap it up. Why did you write this? So what? What do you have to say about it? (last sentence):

_____

_____

Editing Checklist

Directions: Edit your written work using the Self-Edit columns, fixing any errors you notice. Then, ask someone to complete the Peer Edit column.

	Self-Edit		Peer Edit	
	Checklist Items		Checklist Items	
Punctuation	I read my written piece aloud to see where to stop or pause for periods, question marks, exclamation marks, and commas.		I read the author's piece aloud to see where to stop or pause for periods, question marks, exclamation marks, and commas.	
	Quotation marks are included where needed.		Quotation marks are included where needed.	
Capital Letters	I checked for capitals at the beginning of sentences.		I checked for capitals at the beginning of sentences.	
	Proper nouns begin with capital letters.		Proper nouns begin with capital letters.	
Grammar	My sentences are complete thoughts and contain a noun and a verb.		Sentences are complete thoughts and contain a noun and a verb.	
	I don't have any run-on sentences.		There are no run-on sentences.	
Spelling	I checked spelling and fixed the words that didn't look right.		Spelling is correct.	

Checklist is adapted from Read Write Think. Permission is granted to use for educational purposes.

For paragraphs:

_____ Is there an introduction sentence that states the main idea?

_____ Are there at least three details that tell more about the main idea?

_____ Is there a conclusion sentence that wraps up the idea?

Essay Editing Checklist
Organization

Introduction

_____ Introduction begins with an attention grabber or hook.

_____ Introduction has at least three sentences.

_____ Introduction ends with a clear thesis statement.

Body

_____ There are at least three body paragraphs (each indented).

_____ Each body paragraph has a topic sentence.

_____ Each body paragraph has at least three main ideas.

_____ Each body paragraph has a conclusion sentence.

Conclusion

_____ The conclusion paragraph is at least three sentences.

_____ The conclusion paragraph restates the thesis statement.

_____ The conclusion paragraph answers "So what?" or makes a broad generalization.

Coherence

_____ The ideas flow logically and make sense.

_____ Transitions are used correctly.

_____ There are no awkward parts.

_____ The essay is interesting.

Ideas/Content

_____ Everything in the essay supports the thesis statement (main idea).

_____ There is enough supporting evidence for each body paragraph.

_____ Descriptive and precise words are used.

_____ Sentence structure is varied (a mix of simple, compound, and complex sentences).

Grammar and Mechanics

Point out any of the following that you find:

_____ Misspelled words

_____ Grammatical mistakes

_____ Punctuation errors

_____ Run-on Sentences (more than one sentence smooshed together)

_____ Fragments (incomplete sentences)

Adapted and used with permission from Jimmie's Collage.

Writing

Sentences

Writing Sentences 1

Change each sentence to begin with a capital letter and to end with the correct punctuation mark.

1. friday is the best day of the week !

2. i am so excited !

3. why do rainbows come after a rainfall ?

4. come here, now !

5. can I please have a drink ?

6. i don't like spicy food.

7. where are my shoes ?

8. do sea turtles live in seas ?

9. you can do it ! (cheering someone on)

10. gifts are fun to give .

11. rabbits live in dens.

12. do you think rabbits have good hearing ?

For Day 2:
Underline all of the prepositions. Here is a list of some prepositions: of, after, before, on, in, around, by.

Writing Sentences 2

Circle the complete subject and underline the complete predicate. Everything in the sentence should be either circled or underlined.

1. [The little black kitten] is adorable. *Example*

2. (I) like to write stories.

3. (My house) is the third on the left.

4. (The big brown house) is my cousin's.

5. [Living on a farm] is a lot of fun and a lot of work. *Example*

This is a tricky one. We're talking about "living on a farm." That's the subject. An ING noun is called a *gerund.* Sentences 7, 9 and 10 are similar.

6. (All children) love to play.

7. (Reading your Bible) is a good thing to do every day.

8. (Fall) is my favorite season.

9. (Raking leaves) is fun when you get to jump in the leaf pile.

10. (Climbing trees) is a way to have an adventure right at home.

11. (Yummy soup) makes a rainy day better.

12. (I) hope that you have a great day.

Writing Sentences 3

What's missing to make each a correct sentence?

1. My father's friend from school.

2. chores help children learn responsibility.

3. Would you like to come over tomorrow

4. Will be quiet time.

5. Please throw away your trash when you are finished

6. let's go on a picnic for lunch.

7. math is easy when you know the answers.

8. Reading is interesting when you understand

9. People who like to read

10. Over the river and through the woods to Grandmother's house

Writing Sentences 4

If the sentence is correct, place a check mark by it. If not, fix it. Add what is missing to make it a correct sentence. But first, do these first two practices with semicolons.

These sentences should really be two. Split them by adding a semicolon (;). Where does it go?

Please be on time for dinner we are having your favorite.

Writing can be a lot of fun I especially like to write funny stories.

1. Friday is the best day of the week we get to go to the park.

2. That's so exciting!

3. Rainbows after a rainfall

4. No way!

5. I think that's a great idea he will have a great time.

6. Spicy food is the best

7. Where are my shoes

8. Yes!

9. Thanks for coming we appreciate it.

Writing Sentences 5

Write in a proper noun for each common noun. All proper nouns are names and all names are capitalized. What does that mean about proper nouns?

1. house   _____

2. cookie   _____

3. beach   _____

4. theater   _____

5. woman   _____

6. boy   _____

7. store   _____

8. country   _____

9. girl   _____

10. restaurant   _____

Writing Sentences 6

Use a comma and a conjunction (and, but, or) to combine the sentences into one. Just fill in the blanks provided.

Example: Put away your things quickly. Come outside with us to play.

Put away your things quickly, and come outside with us to play.

What happened? The period turned into a comma. The conjunction (connecting word) AND was added, and the capital letter in the second sentence became lower case.

<u>Now You Try</u>

This story is good. The last one was even better.

This story is good _____ last one was even better.

I want to bake a cake. I want to decorate it like a soccer ball.

I want to bake a cake _____ want to decorate it like a soccer ball.

My dog wants to play fetch. Maybe he just wants to be outside.

My dog wants to play fetch _____ he just wants to be outside.

It's fun playing with my cousins when they visit. It's even more fun having siblings to play with every day.

It's fun playing with my cousins when they visit _____ even more fun having siblings to play with every day.

I have a great chocolate cake recipe. I make it for everyone's birthday.

I have a great chocolate cake recipe _____ make it for everyone's birthday.

Please stay in line. We won't be able to get through.

Please stay in line _____ won't be able to get through.

Writing Sentences 7

Finish the sentences using the conjunction noted. Make sure you put a comma before the conjunction.

(FOR) I hope that you have fun today _____

_____

(NOR) I didn't see her today _____

_____

(YET) Playing soccer is a lot of fun _____

_____

(SO) I want to go home _____

_____

Now write your own.

(AND) _____

_____

(BUT) _____

_____

(OR) _____

_____

Writing Sentences 8
Commas

Add in commas where they are needed. They aren't needed in every sentence!
Commas go in lists, between date words, and between date numbers.

1. Please go get me a pencil a piece of paper scissors and glue.

2. Christmas is on December 25 every year.

3. My grandfather was born on December 8 1941.

4. My chores are to clear the table put away the shoes organize the toys and take cups to the kitchen.

5. The birthday party invitation says it's on Saturday November 11th.

6. My birthday will be on Monday this year.

7. I'm going to be visiting my relatives in April 2015.

8. My brothers' names are Matthew Mark Luke and John.

9. It's so loud outside because they are digging up the concrete.

10. I really want to go but I don't have a ticket.

Writing Sentences 9
Capitalization

Circle the letters that should be capitalized. Remember, all names should be capitalized: names of people, names of places and names of things. What else should be capitalized? (Then go back and underline the prepositions: by, in, on, after, before, at, for, into, up, down, about, through, around, near, nearby, to.)

1. my family took a trip to washington, d.c. and saw the lincoln memorial.

2. suzanna lives on blueberry lane near the post office in middletown.

3. subway sells sandwiches in north and south america, europe, asia and africa.

4. there are many places around the world where you can buy chocolate chip cookies.

5. saint basil's cathedral is in red square in moscow, russia.

6. the grand canyon was visited last year by five thousand people named joshua.

7. the star spangled banner by francis scott key was written after a battle in the war of 1812.

8. we visited the empire state building when we took a trip to new york.

9. dr. george's address is 702 hancock way, newford, connecticut.

10. matthew, mark, luke and john are the four gospels found in the new testament.

Writing Sentences 10

Circle the letters that need to be capitalized. Add in the missing commas.

<u>New rules</u>: Unimportant words in titles aren't capitalized and place names are separated with commas, such as Springfield, Michigan or Paris, France.

1. i need you to be in smallsville north dakota on monday august 14th.

2. remember to bring your notebook a snack to share and your book.

3. november 1 2001 was abigail's birthday and every year I tell the story of when she was born.

4. philadelphia pennsylvania usa is known as the city of brotherly love.

5. i love this song and i especially love it when my friend sings it.

6. today we're going to ride our bikes play a board game and make welcome home signs.

7. our plane to helsinki finland leaves on monday july 30th at 5:00 AM.

8. amy carmichael was from Ireland but she was a missionary in dohnavur india.

9. *clay* is the title of the book my brother wrote.

10. king david actually wrote the words to many of the songs we sing in church because he wrote the psalms we get them from.

Writing Sentences 11

Choose the pronoun that belongs. Circle the correct pronoun for the sentence.

Object pronouns: me, him, her, us, them

1. Caroline and (me I) are going outside to play.

2. Get a drink for all of (them they).

3. The prize goes to (her she).

4. There's a surprise inside for all of (us we).

5. The book was a present to Sarah and (me I).

6. Give (him he) the paper.

7. When we get older, Samuel and (me I) are going to open a pizza restaurant.

8. I hope that Rachel and (me I) both get chosen to be in the play.

9. Just when I thought it was safe, my little brother barreled around the corner and plowed right into my sister and (me I).

10. I'm saving up money to get a remote control car for (him he) and a paint set for (her she).

Writing Sentences 12

Fill in the pronoun that best fits the blank. Sometimes it could be more than one (for instance: him or her).

subject pronoun: I, you, he, she, it, we, you, they
object pronoun: me, you, him, her, it, us, you, them

1. Caroline and _____ are going outside to play.

2. Get a drink for all of _____.

3. The prize goes to _____.

4. There's a surprise inside for all of _____.

5. The book was a present to Sarah and _____.

6. That story was written by Paul and _____.

7. When we get older, Samuel and _____ are going to open a pizza restaurant.

8. I hope that Rachel and _____ both get chosen to be in the play.

9. Just when I thought it was safe, my little brother barreled around the corner and plowed right into my sister and _____.

10. I'm saving up money to get a remote control car for _____ and a paint set for _____.

Writing Sentences 13

Fill in the correct form of the word.

it's : It's means it is. It's snowing outside. Say, "It is."
its : Its is a possessive pronoun. Its lid is on the counter. Its is followed by a noun.

their : T-H-E-I-R is the possessive adjective. That is their house. That is their dog.
     Their is followed by a noun.
there : T-H-E-R-E is the word when you are showing where something is. It's over there.
     There refers to a place.
they're : T-H-E-Y-'-R-E is a contraction. It means they are. They're the ones who are helping.
     Say "they are" to see if this is what is needed in the sentence.

1. Christina, _____ snowing outside!

2. Your drink is over _____.

3. Be careful. _____ lid is off.

4. There's a surprise in _____ for all of us.

5. The book was _____ present.

6. _____ going to work together to deliver the papers.

7. When they get older, _____ going to open a restaurant.

8. I hope _____ going to be fun.

9. I didn't notice the wires, and I tripped over _____ cord.

10. Do you have _____ phone number?

11. I volunteered to walk _____dog while _____ away.

12. _____ leash is kept over _____ by the door.

_____ red.

Writing Sentences 14

Lie vs. Lay
Circle the correct word for each sentence.

To lie means to recline.
To lay means to put down.

1. I will just lie/lay here until you are ready.

2. He lies/lays out his supplies very carefully before he begins his work.

3. He lies/lays out his cars all in a row.

4. I will lie/lay the baby down for his nap.

5. He is just lying/laying there.

6. I've trained her to lie/lay still until called.

7. Please lie/lay the photograph back on the shelf when you are done looking at it.

8. The baby is lying/laying in her crib.

9. Lie/Lay it right here.

10. Never tell a _____ .

Writing Sentences 15
Past Tense

Fill in the correct past tense form of the verb in parentheses.

1. We made pudding and a membrane _____ (lie) over its top after it cooled.

2. I came in and _____ (lay) my book right here. Where is it?

3. He spilled when he _____ (pour) himself a cup of milk.

4. I _____ (run) home as fast as I could.

5. I _____ (hope) that I would be here when he got home.

6. He _____ (hit) the ball over the fence.

7. I _____ (read) that book before.

8. We _____ (have) that same problem.

9. She _____ (ring) the doorbell.

10. They _____ (throw) me a congratulations party.

11. He was so sore after practice he just _____ (lie) prone the rest of the day.

Writing Sentences 16

Circle the letters that should be capitalized in the titles listed below. A title is the name of a thing: a book, a song, a movie, etc. There are a few differences though in how we capitalize a title. We capitalize the first and last words always. We capitalize most words, but we leave lowercase insignificant words like "the" and "a" and most prepositions (those words we've been practicing this year such as in, on, between, from, of, at, and about).

joy to the world

the king will make a way

silent night

the boxcar children

this little light of mine

easy peasy all-in-one homeschool

horton hears a who

the cat and the hat

rock of ages

abc world news tonight

alexander and the terrible, horrible, no good, very bad day

Now try some in sentences. Find ALL the letters that should be capitalized.

mary left her book, *little house on the prairie*, in pennsylvania.

martin luther king, jr. sang the song *hark the herald angels sing* at the first baptist church on oak street. (There are 13 capital letters in this one!)

Writing Sentences 17

Place a comma after the introductory phrase.

1. After we get home from the store everyone will help put things away.

2. If we win we will get to go to the championship game.

3. When it rains we always get a big puddle in our yard.

4. Under the ocean in the amazing coral reef there live thousands of unique sea creatures.

5. Raising her hand high Stephanie was sure she knew the answer.

6. When we are ready to go we'll pack the van.

7. Getting her cast off Riley was finally able to run around again with her siblings.

8. If someone comes to the door come and get me.

9. If you need any help please ask.

10. When you receive a compliment say thank you like you would if you had been given a gift.

11. Placing the application in the mailbox Matthew prayed he would get the job.

12. In just another minute or two we'll be done.

Writing Sentences 18

Now you are going to take the comma out of the sentences. Rewrite the sentences with no comma. They are all wrong! For one, never, ever separate a subject from its verb with just one comma. The Answer Book has explanations for why the commas are incorrect in each sentence.

1. Raking leaves, is a fun job, when you get to jump in the leaves.

_____

_____

2. I really like to play the game Pit, because it can get really loud and wild.

_____

_____

3. It's fun to play in the snow, if you have a warm house to go back to.

_____

_____

4. Building a snowman and dressing him up, is a favorite winter activity.

_____

_____

5. I like to ride bikes, and jump rope.

_____

_____

Writing Sentences 19

Place the quotation marks and commas where they belong. Some of the commas have been added as examples. Use them to help you figure out the others.

Examples: "Let me show you," she said.
He said, "Please come with us."

1. Come home right after supper, Dad instructed.

2. Did you forget to bring your bag? Mom asked.

3. I'll go to the store first, Sarah said, and then I'll come right home.

4. Mark answered, I like the color green best.

5. Wait for me! Stephanie yelled.

6. Wait just a minute Paul begged and I'll be able to go with you.

7. Dave questioned What about me?

8. Bethany said Saturday is usually the best time to get together.

9. I think I figured it out said Nathaniel with excitement. The puzzle fits together this way.

Make observations about capitalization.
Rewrite this sentence correctly.

Elizabeth wanted to go, so she said, "let me come too!"

_____

Make observations about the placement of commas.
Rewrite this sentence correctly. Fix both commas.

"Please excuse me", Andrew said politely ", while I get what we need."

_____

Writing Sentences 20

Place commas where they belong. Three sentences don't need any commas. Three sentences need only one comma.

1. "After we get home from the store everyone will help put things away" my mom reminded us.

2. Inspired with a great idea Ned set off to write out his plan.

3. "If we win we will get to go to the championship game" she explained.

4. On December 7 1941 Pearl Harbor was attacked.

5. Raking leaves is a fun job when you get to jump in the leaves.

6. Thinking through everything she needed to buy she made a list that included paper plates flour lemons and straws.

7. Putting away the dishes she was thankful for a full house.

8. I really like to play the game Pit because it can get really loud and wild.

9. It's fun to play in the snow if you have a warm house to go back to.

10. "If you think it is necessary send a letter to the group in Detroit Michigan as well" Mary decided.

11. When it rains we always get a big puddle in our yard.

Here are two sentences with extra information. Put commas around it. I'll give you one example first.

Example: Louise, the first girl I ever knew to play baseball, was a fast pitcher. This gives extra information about Louise. The information comes immediately after the noun it's describing. You could take out the words between the commas and the sentence would still work. Try it!

Doug the only one wearing a hat was best prepared for the trip.

Riley was a gymnast someone who can flip and fly and twist and balance.

Spelling Review

Spelling Review 1

Unscramble the words and solve the puzzle by filling in the blanks with the numbered letters. You can also use the puzzle to help you unscramble the words.

__ **N** __ __ __   __ __ __ __ __ __ __ __ __
1 2 3 4 5   6 7 8 9 10 11 12 13 14

SAONES   S E A S O N (example)
                                      2

SOSFRMEL   __ __ __ __ __ __ __ __
                                        7

DRAKSNES   __ __ __ __ __ __ __ __
                                        13

VINGOM   __ __ __ __ __ __
                                            8

TSIDM   __ __ __ __ __
                             9

TEAPEARS   __ __ __ __ __ __ __ __
                                         3

BOTGUHR   __ __ __ __ __ __ __
                                      4

VENGETTIOA   __ __ __ __ __ __ __ __ __ __
                                                   10

IBRGAEN   __ __ __ __ __ __ __
                                   11

HTBREA   __ __ __ __ __ __
            6

LHGTI   __ __ __ __ __
                12

NEVAHE   __ __ __ __ __ __
          5

GSIN   __ __ __ __
        1   14

Need help? brought, darkness, light, breath, midst, formless, separate, moving, vegetation, sign, heaven, bearing

Spelling Review 2

Lay a piece of paper over the blank part of this page and write as many of these spelling words as you can. Use a pen and press down firmly. Then scribble over the blank page with a pencil to reveal your words.

creatures, fruitful, cattle, ground, beast, multiply, kind, creep

Spelling Review 3

Find the words listed below and circle them in the puzzle. The can be found forward and backward, vertically, horizontally, and diagonally.

```
W  U  D  I  X  V  G  V  B  Z  H  N  F  V  C  D
N  X  N  O  I  T  A  E  R  C  N  O  K  H  F  R
V  P  L  N  J  O  H  Z  P  P  F  S  K  P  F  E
R  J  Y  R  A  S  W  M  H  Q  Y  T  F  L  V  F
A  Z  A  D  X  D  I  B  G  N  K  R  L  P  E  K
H  L  L  R  E  Q  E  N  P  H  M  I  Z  U  D  Q
K  T  Y  D  E  H  I  T  T  G  M  L  K  P  E  V
X  R  S  Q  B  E  T  N  U  O  X  S  G  Y  T  U
L  L  E  H  B  Y  E  A  V  O  V  O  Y  H  E  W
Y  I  A  K  R  V  B  H  E  O  R  K  P  O  L  I
N  K  R  U  E  U  A  J  S  R  C  P  E  T  P  X
P  C  T  S  H  F  B  L  O  T  B  F  S  J  M  G
L  A  H  S  A  S  M  E  C  A  F  R  U  S  O  P
K  F  K  T  N  E  Q  D  G  T  G  I  C  M  C  H
D  Y  Z  Q  Z  Z  U  R  U  W  L  Z  Y  E  C  K
F  J  I  O  T  C  Z  S  U  B  D  U  E  T  S  V
```

- completed
- subdue
- sprouted
- seventh
- surface
- sky
- nostrils
- earth
- being
- shrub
- creation
- breathed

Spelling Review 4   Cut out the word parts. Can you line them up in the right order? Here's a hint: it starts with IMP.

imp   thr   entf

our   lem   eas

nfi   ult   iva

tet   onc   hir

dga   rde   eldr

rsl   ive   ept

Need help? cultivate, garden, implement, fourth, third, river, field, slept, reason

Spelling Review 5

Directions: Fill in your spelling words to make them all fit in the above puzzle. Here is your word list and some hints to get you started. Hint: Count the number of spaces and the lengths of the words and match them up.

direction, wanderer, field, blood, great, driven, vagrant, vengeance, father, dwell, tents birth, lyre, implements, speech, striking

Spelling Review 6

Use your Day 40 spelling words as your path from start to finish. One false move and... Just kidding. Nothing will happen to you. The word path can twist and turn but will never go in a diagonal. I cleared the beginning of the path to get you started. Use a pencil to trace your path. Have fun!

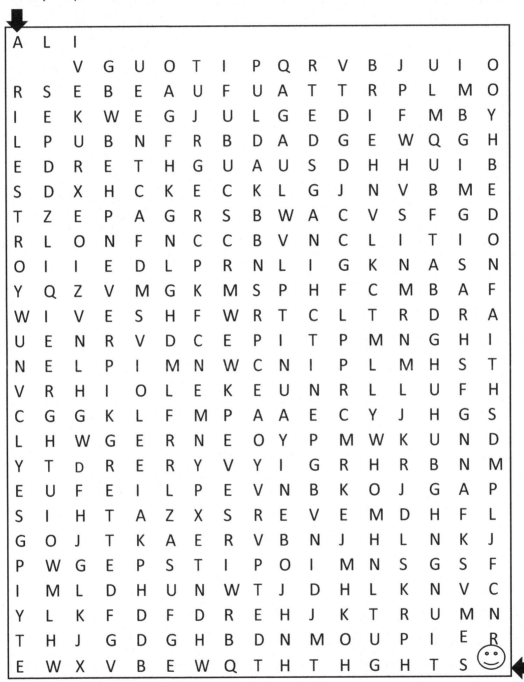

beautiful, daughter, whomever, inclination, regretted, faithfully, thoughts, violence, pitch, destroy, wives, alive, seven, hundredth

Spelling Review 7

This is a different kind of unscramble puzzle. The letters below each column each go in one of the boxes above it. Words are written across in rows. The columns in the puzzle DO NOT spell anything. Once you write in a word, cross the used letters off underneath. Hint: Match the length of words and the number of boxes.

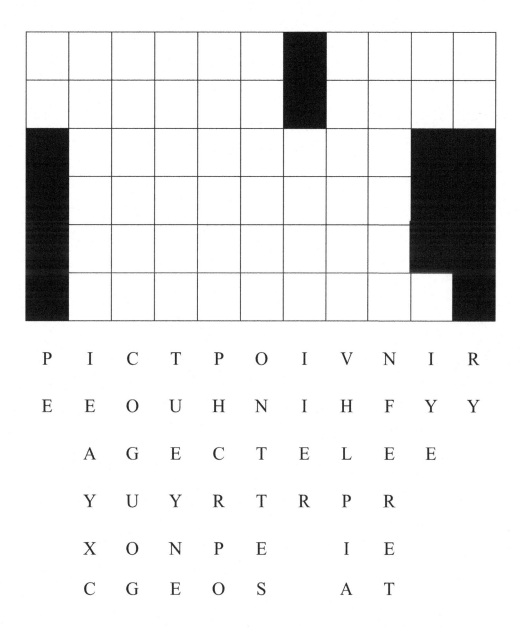

P	I	C	T	P	O	I	V	N	I	R
E	E	O	U	H	N	I	H	F	Y	Y
A	G	E	C	T	E	L	E	E		
Y	U	Y	R	T	R	P	R			
X	O	N	P	E		I	E			
C	G	E	O	S		A	T			

Need help? shield, Egyptian, heir, pigeon, priest, sandal, enemies, except, heir, prey, children, Egyptian, conceive, maid, authority, against, east, yourself

Spelling Review 8

Cut out the 42 word parts and have someone hide them for you or each takes some and hide them for each other. Piece together your spelling words from Day 50.

jour   ney   ed

ed   ed   ter

tho   scat   rou

ghly   ess   bui

ing   poss   ld

ed   ions   ed

wom   acq

uir   an   hed

pitc   don   pt

keys   Egy   ong

esc   ort   bel

num   ber   ly

form   er   exc

eed   ing   ly

Need help? journeyed, scattered, thoroughly, building, possessions, acquired, pitched, donkeys, woman, Egypt, escorted, belonged, number, formerly, exceedingly

Spelling Review 9

Directions:

This is like the game Battleship.

Players write five words on their board, one letter per square. The words can go top to bottom and left to right. Words can intersect (share a letter, like in a crossword puzzle).

Players take turns guessing a square by naming its number and letter position. The other player must say either that it is blank or the letter in the square. If that square is blank, the player can place a dot or X in the square on the "opponent's" board to mark that it's been guessed already. If the square is not, the letter should be written in the square on the "opponent's" board.

After setting up your "ship" words, you don't need to write on your board again during the game. You just keep track of the game on the "opponent's" board. When you are asked about a square, you will check and tell what's in the square on the "My Ships" board.

The winner is the first to find all the letters of all five words on the opponent's board, in other words, to sink the opponent's word ships.

MY OPPONENT'S SHIPS

	1	2	3	4	5	6	7	8	9
A									
B									
C									
D									
E									
F									
G									
H									
I									

Day 45 words: decreased, mountains, subsided, recede, require, families, dried, cease, aroma, account, covenant

MY SHIPS

	1	2	3	4	5	6	7	8	9
A									
B									
C									
D									
E									
F									
G									
H									
I									

Spelling Review 10

Cut out the word strips and place them in a pile upside down. Choose someone to be the "spell checker." Take turns choosing a word from the pile and spelling it. Older kids can hand their word to the spell checker without looking (or just have the spell checker pick it up) and will have the word read to them. Middle kids could look at the word and then give it to the "spell checker." Younger children could keep the word in front of them while they spell. You will stand and spell the word out loud. When you say a tall letter (t, h, f, d, b, l, k), reach both hands all the way up. When you say a hanging letter (y, p, g, j), touch your toes. Otherwise, put your hands on your hips.

throughout

foreigner

twelve

ninety-nine

appeared

opposite

bowed

measure

denied

advanced

appointed

difficult

righteousness

command

judge

forty-five

Spelling Review 11

Find the words hidden in the puzzle. There are no diagonal words.

Day 75 Spelling Words

```
U R G E D L Q R E M E M B E R
T K R G D H L A S C E N D W I
N T C L E L Z A V W P C R E W
E O G S U W W N N E X G R Z
M W E T Q X L R S M O K E M U
H A S N I L Z C W L W H B Z L
S R C A N S U P I L L A R P V
I D A T H W I V P G B O W R U
N P P I C S U R R O U N D E D
U C E B E P W X R R R A T S K
P Z T A T T Q J S D A D V E N
H V O H R Z B C A S I D L R W
Q Q C N V E O X O U F Q L V A
Y R W I B R A I N E D I J E D
N Q Z E L Z V U F S E I Z E Q
```

TOWARD	ASCEND	DAWN	ESCAPE	INHABITANTS
PILLAR	PRESERVE	PUNISHMENT	REMEMBER	SEIZE
SURROUNDED	TECHNIQUE	URGED	SMOKE	RAINED

Spelling Review 12

Unscramble the words and solve the puzzle by filling in the blanks with the numbered letters. You can also use the puzzle to help you unscramble the words.

___ _Y_ ___   ___ ___ ___ ___ ___ ___ ___   ___ ___ _V_ ___ ___
1   2   3   4   5   6   7   8   9   10   11 12 13 14 15

NIRHFTEG   ___ ___ ___ ___ ___ ___ ___ ___
                  3

NEONECCIN   ___ ___ ___ ___ ___ ___ ___ ___ ___
                                              6

REPOHTP   ___ ___ ___ ___ ___ ___ ___
                            14

NOTNAI   ___ ___ ___ ___ ___ ___
                      12

BOMW   ___ ___ ___ ___
              1&8

EWRNDA   ___ ___ ___ ___ ___ ___
                            10

RATELGUH   ___ ___ ___ ___ ___ ___ ___ ___
              11

SIACA   ___ ___ ___ ___ ___
              15

DEANEW   ___ ___ ___ ___ ___ ___
                            5

CISPEE   ___ ___ ___ ___ ___ ___
                  4

BONRE   ___ ___ ___ ___ ___
                        7

SINTEL   ___ ___ ___ ___ ___ ___
                        9

Need help? die, angel, thousand, pieces, frighten, Isaac, weaned, borne, maid, innocence, prophet, wander, listen, laughter, nation, womb

Spelling Review 13   Directions are on Spelling Review 9, but this time use 7 words.

MY OPPONENT'S SHIPS

A									
B									
C									
D									
E									
F									
G									
H									
I									
	1	2	3	4	5	6	7	8	9

Day 85: swear, falsely, army, ewe, complain, oath, son, said, there, lamb, burnt, worship, knife

MY SHIPS

A									
B									
C									
D									
E									
F									
G									
H									
I									
	1	2	3	4	5	6	7	8	9

Spelling Review 14

Correct the misspelled words. Maybe there is a letter missing. Or maybe there is an incorrect letter used. Write out the correct spelling of the word. Words are from Day 90.

strech   _____

cought   _____

agenst   _____

thiket   _____

provid   _____

mownt   _____

declair   _____

tecknology   _____

secind   _____

seeshore   _____

Write the homophone.

to, too   _____

would   _____

ate   _____

Write the plural. The last one is a bonus. ☺

child _____ woman _____

mouse _____ cactus _____

Spelling Review 15

The letter may be missing from more than one spot. Words are from Day 95.

Fill in the missing U's.

BRIAL

_____

BRYING

_____

FOR

_____

HNDRED

_____

Fill in the missing A's.

PPROCH

_____

NSWER

_____

STNDRD

_____

Fill in the missing I's.

COMMERCAL

_____

SGHT

_____

PRCE

_____

WEGH

_____

SATSFED

_____

Fill in the missing O's.

PEPLE

_____

WRTH

_____

CNFINES

_____

Spelling Review 16

Use the words listed from Day 110 as your path from start to finish. One false move and... Just kidding. Nothing will happen to you. The word path can twist and turn but will never go in a diagonal. I cleared the beginning of the path to get you started. Use a pencil to trace your path and to cross out words you've already found. Have fun!

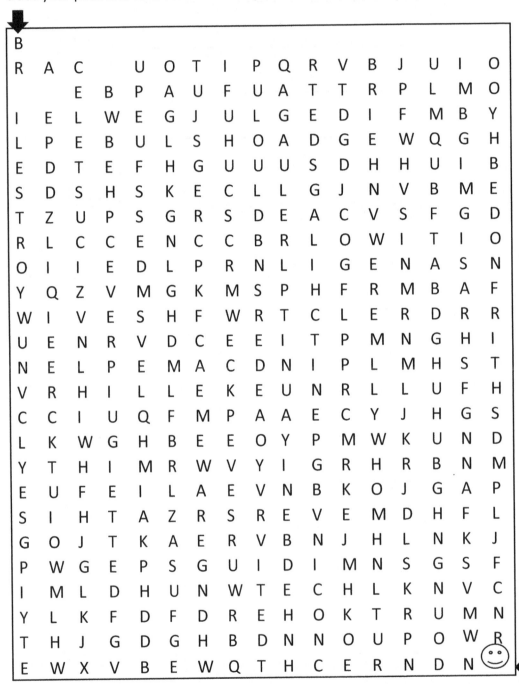

thigh, beware, concern, quickly, lower, shoulder, emptied, camel, guide, bracelet, successful, down

Spelling Review 17

Cut out the word parts and join them together to make a list of some of your spelling words from Day 115. I'll give you a hint. It starts with GRI.

gri   efia   cen

vie   ddes   ddec

eit   fuld   ncev

sol   efen   entl

iol   ycon   eflo

tle   ckw   res

Need help? embrace, grief, defiance, thirty-seven, console, deceitful, flock, descend, almond, continue, distance, gracious, envied, prevail, wrestle, violently (not all words are used)

Spelling Review 18 Directions are on Spelling Review 9, but this time use 6 words.

MY OPPONENT'S SHIPS

A									
B									
C									
D									
E									
F									
G									
H									
I									
	1	2	3	4	5	6	7	8	9

Day 120: bind, erect, rebuke, pasture, welfare, devour, rescue, further, balm, myrrh, caravan

MY SHIPS

A									
B									
C									
D									
E									
F									
G									
H									
I									
	1	2	3	4	5	6	7	8	9

Spelling Review 19

Cut out the word strips and place them in a pile upside down. Choose someone to be the "spell checker." Take turns choosing a word from the pile and spelling it. Older kids can hand their word to the spell checker without looking (or just have the spell checker pick it up) and will have the word read to them. Middle kids could look at the word and then give it to the "spell checker." Younger children could keep the word in front of them while they spell. You will stand and spell the word out loud. When you say a tall letter (t, h, f, d, b, l, k), reach both hands all the way up. When you say a hanging letter (y, p, g, j), touch your toes. Otherwise, put your hands on your hips.

officer

desire

appearance

handsome

garment

Hebrew

fled

jailer

extend

charge

anger

furious

officials

baker

confinement

Spelling Review 20

What letter is missing? In each group, the same letter is missing from each word. The missing letter may appear more than once in a word. Write out the correct words. If you need help, these words are from Day 130.

ort   baket   talk   ubequent

_____

sort, basket, talks, subsequent

sorh   aptain   hief   exat

_____

scorch, captain, chief, exact

famie   iform   ukow   discer

_____

famine, inform, unknow, discern

fvorbly   mgicin   proposl   bundnce

_____

favorably, magician, proposal, abundance

Grammar Review

Grammar Review 2 – Prepositional Phrases

Underline the prepositional phrase. Circle the object of the preposition. Put a line over the preposition.

> I did just one in the first sentence for you, but I can't draw an over line. Prepositions are locaters: ON the desk, IN the desk, UNDER the desk, BESIDE the desk, AT the desk, BY the desk, TO the desk, TOWARD the desk, etc.

> Two more prepositions that you'll see a lot are the words OF and FOR.

1. I wish I could take a walk across the ocean under the starry sky and above the confused fish.

2. I bought some Indian tea and drank it in my china cup that I got in Florida.

3. The knight stormed the gates of the castle and freed the prisoners.

4. I went to Italy and saw the Leaning Tower of Pisa, but unfortunately, I sneezed too hard and knocked it over.

5. We rode in a glass-bottom boat, so we could see the colorful fish swimming under us.

6. I want to break the world's record for the biggest statue made of raisins.

Grammar Review 3 – Direct Objects

I have highlighted the verb that has the direct object for you to find. Underline the object. The direct object answers the question, what, in response to an action verb.

Example: I gave the book to my daughter. Gave is the verb. Book is the direct object. What did I give her? the book

1. I wish I could take a walk across the ocean under the starry sky and above the confused fish.

2. I bought some Indian tea and drank it in my china cup that I got in Florida.

3. The knight stormed the gates of the castle and freed the prisoners.

4. I went to Italy and saw the Leaning Tower of Pisa, but unfortunately, I sneezed too hard and knocked it over.

5. We rode in a glass-bottom boat, so we could see the colorful fish swimming under us.

6. I want to break the world's record for the biggest statue made out of raisins.

Grammar Review 4

Directions: Are the highlighted nouns objects of prepositions or direct objects? Circle the prepositions or underline the verbs in each sentence that go with the marked objects.

1. On the way to the park, I found a coin.

2. Get your coat off the floor, please.

3. I need a tissue.

4. Let's take the train into the city.

5. The computer is on the desk.

6. I'm writing the story in my notebook.

7. Pass the ketchup, please.

8. Let's make happy birthday posters.

9. She did a great job at the competition.

10. Let's eat pizza for dinner.

Grammar Review 6

Write the appropriate type of word into each blank. Then read the story with your words inserted. This is like Mad Libs.

_____1. adjective

_____2. action verb

_____3. same verb in the past tense (write it like it happened yesterday)

_____4. adjective

_____5. plural noun (plural means more than one, like apples, with an S)

_____6. possessive adjective (my, your, its, our, their)

_____7. adjective

_____8. noun

_____9. adjective

_____10. noun

_____11. action verb in the past tense

_____12. noun, body part

_____13. noun, used for action in number 2 (ex. run, sneakers)

_____14. noun

_____15. adjective, number

_____16. plural noun, length of time

_____17. action verb, past tense

_____18. adjective

_____19. noun, common noun for who does action in number 2

_____20. proper noun, name of someone who does the action in #2

Grammar Review 7

Correct the mistakes. Correct verb forms, capitalization, punctuation, and word choice where you see problems. There can be more than one way to fix some problems. I found 12 mistakes. How many can you find?

I love running, I try to run Every day. I run with my dog and it's

the two of we out together on the road. I run on chimpmunk lane

and then to the park. Yesterday I run all the way to walmart.

when I run, I like to hum. Humming songs makes it more fun for I.

Do you like to run. Its a good way to exercise.

Grammar Review 8

Correct the mistakes. Correct verb forms, capitalization, punctuation, and word choice where you see problems. There can be more than one way to fix some problems. I found 14 mistakes. How many can you find?

Sarah is my friends. We like to lay in the grass and watch the

clouds. We saw a cloud that she thought looked like a turtle and I

thought that it looked like a snail. Clouds are fascinating. Did you

know that their made of water. there in the sky they float along as

the wind pushes they. She and me also like to make lemonade.

We squeeze the lemons add water and sugar and stir. I think all

childs like to make lemonade. do you

Grammar Review 9

This story is missing all punctuation and capitalization! Circle each letter that should be capitalized and write in all other punctuation.

please follow all of the instructions said the teacher i want to make sure everyone knows what to do nathan was the first to finish and he raised his hand

yes nathan

im finished he said what should i do now

why don't you help someone else

looking around nathan noticed grace had made a cool design on her project if i help you with the folding will you draw that design on mine too

Grammar Review 10

All of the capitalization and punctuation is missing! Circle every letter that should be capitalized and write in all of the punctuation.

our family was on a trip to washington dc I had never been before and i was really excited on our first day there monday may 4 2015 we could have gone inside but we weren't allowed we decided to head to the lincoln memorial where there is a huge statue of abraham lincoln then we went up the washington monument if you ever go to washington you should do that too

Vocabulary Review

Vocabulary Review 1 Days 1-25

Match the words ~~with their~~ definitions by writing the letter of the correct definition in the blan~~k~~

	A.	to bring under control
___2. void	B.	completely empty
___3. midst	C.	to take materials and make them into something
___4. mist	D.	to separate into parts
___5. subdue	E.	to move slowly and carefully to avoid notice
___6. divide	F.	a low lying cloud
___7. dimension	G.	being there
___8. presence	H.	to mind others
___9. swarm	I.	to rule, to be in control over a group of people
___10. cultivate	J.	in the middle of
___11. my brother's keeper	K.	measurement, or an aspect of something
___12. enmity	L.	clever at using deception to get what you want
___13. implement	M.	tool made for a particular use
___14. expanse	N.	hatred
___15. crafty	O.	a person who wanders from place to place
___16. fashion	P.	to abound, teem, to be overrun
___17. govern	Q.	to produce
___18. creep	R.	to prepare and use land for crops
___19. vagrant	S.	to put someone in position in a particular place
___20. station	T.	a large, wide, open area of land or water

Vocabulary Review 2

Tell a story. One person begins. Their turn ends when they use the next word in a sentence. Then the next person picks up the story and continues until they can use the next word in a sentence.

1   void – completely empty
2   expanse – a large, wide, open area of land or water
3   yield – to produce
4   govern – to rule, to be in control over a group of people
5   swarm – to abound, teem, to be overrun
6   creep – to move slowly and carefully, especially to avoid notice
7   dimension – measurement, or an aspect of something
8   subdue – to bring under control
9   mist – a low lying cloud
10   midst – in the middle of
11   divide – to separate into parts
12   cultivate -- to prepare and use land for crops
13   fashion – to take materials and make them into something
14   crafty, shrewd, vulpine -- clever at using deception to get what you want
15   enmity – hatred, being actively opposed to someone or something
16   station – to put someone in a position in a particular place for a particular purpose
17   my brother's keeper – to mind others
18   vagrant – a person who wanders from place to place, living by begging
19   presence – being there, whether seen or not, or a group or people all together in a particular place for a particular reason, or an impact made by being there
20   implement – tool made for a particular use, put a plan into action

Across

2. Keep a cheerful <u>countenance</u>.

4. I lost him in the _____ of the crowd.

6. It may seem the sky is _____, but it is filled with billions of objects.

8. I have never learned to properly _____ the land in order to grow a better garden.

9. We _____ a small fort out of the lumber we had stored behind the house.

13. The bees _____ after their attacker.

15. The heavens are an _____ above the earth.

17. The trees _____ fruit for our family.

18. God created seeds and caused the ground _____ the plants and shrubs and trees. *This answer is three words. Add a space between each word.

19. A king should _____ his people justly.

Down

1. God created so many different kinds of water animals; the waters _____ with life.

3. _____ these cookies up evenly among everyone.

5. I'll _____ you by the door so you can welcome the guests.

7. Satan is _____ and tries to confuse us about the truth of God's word.

10. This spot is _____ for a picnic.

11. There is _____ between the people of God and the works of Satan.

12. Andrew likes to _____ along the floor behind the couch, hoping to go unnoticed.

13. If a lion escaped from a zoo, they would have to _____ it in order to bring it back.

14. I walked through the cool _____ on my early morning walk.

16. God has _____ His people.

If you need help, you can look at the vocabulary review list from your Vocabulary Review 1.

Vocabulary Review 3

Charades
Take turns choosing a word on the list to act out. You can also use the list to guess what words others are acting out.

strive - struggle

corrupt - willing to do something wrong

establish - to create something

righteous - doing what is right

recede - to go back

abate - to lessen

intent - purpose

successive - coming after another

mortar - used to bind bricks

accumulate - gather

severe - intense

sustain - support

array - dress someone

iniquity - sin

obtain - to get

affliction - suffering

intercept - blocking something from where it's going

tender - easy to chew

appointed - designated

venture - to do something daring

strive		severe
corrupt		sustain
establish		array
righteous	Vocabulary Review 4&5, Grammar Review 5	iniquity
recede		obtain
abate		affliction
intent		intercept
successive		tender
mortar		appointed
accumulate		venture

struggle	intense
willing to do something wrong	support
to create something	dress someone
doing what is right	sin
to go back	to get
to lessen	suffering
purpose	blocking something
coming after another	easy to chew
used to bind bricks	designated
gather	to do something daring

Vocabulary Review 6

1. omniscient
A.   being shown innocent of an accusation of wrong doing
B.   the character quality of holding to strong moral principles
C.   to gradually get used to not having something you've become dependent on
D.   all knowing

2. integrity
A.   to take hold of suddenly and forcibly
B.   being shown innocent of an accusation of wrong doing
C.   to gradually get used to not having something you've become dependent on
D.   the character quality of holding to strong moral principles

3. altar
A.   to take hold of suddenly and forcibly
B.   to state clearly, to make known publicly
C.   an elevated surface where religious rites are performed
D.   the character quality of holding to strong moral principles

4. posterity
A.   being shown innocent of an accusation of wrong doing
B.   to state clearly, to make known publicly
C.   a person's descendants or all future generations
D.   to go up

5. jest
A.   to take hold of suddenly and forcibly
B.   to speak or act jokingly
C.   being shown innocent of an accusation of wrong doing
D.   the character quality of holding to strong moral principles

6. seize
A.   an elevated surface where religious rites are performed
B.   to take hold of suddenly and forcibly
C.   to state clearly, to make known publicly
D.   to feel deeply saddened over a loss

7. declare

A.   to state clearly, to make known publicly

B.   the character quality of holding to strong moral principles

C.   a person's descendants or all future generations

D.   like a wife but doesn't have the rights of a wife

8. mourn

A.   like a wife but doesn't have the rights of a wife

B.   an elevated surface where religious rites are performed

C.   to gradually get used to not having something you've become dependent on

D.   to feel deeply saddened over a loss

9. ascend

A.   the character quality of holding to strong moral principles

B.   to go up

C.   a person's descendants or all future generations

D.   to gradually get used to not having something you've become dependent on

10. vindication

A.   to take hold of suddenly and forcibly

B.   to state clearly, to make known publicly

C.   like a wife but doesn't have the rights of a wife

D.   being shown innocent of an accusation of wrong doing

11. wean

A.   to state clearly, to make known publicly

B.   like a wife but doesn't have the rights of a wife

C.   an elevated surface where religious rites are performed

D.   to gradually get used to not having something you've become dependent on

Vocabulary Review 7

This paragraph is all mixed up. Can you put the vocabulary words in their correct places?

We were <u>distressed</u> to sign up for this field trip. It is an excellent <u>soujourner</u>; we were getting a free tour of the colonial house. The guides don't do the tours for <u>inhabitant</u> purposes. They just enjoy it. As we <u>arose</u> the property, we passed a <u>standard</u>. The stone house <u>urged</u> from behind a small hill. The house had no <u>thicket</u>. I asked if I could be a <u>offering</u> there. We were <u>approached</u> to learn that the colonial house needed repairs to remain up to <u>commercial</u>. We were happy to give a donation to help them.

We were _____ to sign up for this field trip. It is an

excellent _____; we were getting a free tour of the

colonial house. The guides don't do the tours for _____

purposes. They just enjoy it. As we _____ the property,

we   passed   a   _____.   The   stone   house

_____ from behind a small hill. The house had no

_____. I asked if I could be a _____

there. We were _____ to learn that the colonial house

needed repairs to remain up to _____. We were happy

to give a donation to help them.

Vocabulary Review 8

Choose a word to either act out or to draw. Take turns at guessing. Keep choosing new words.

concerning – related to a subject

adverb – word that describes how something is done

lodge – to stay a short time in a place such as a home or hotel

envy – jealousy; being upset over what someone else has and you don't

deceit – the act of lying

feeble – weak

droves – a large crowd

prevail – to win, to be widespread or more frequently occurring

rebuke – to scold; to sharply tell someone their behavior is wrong

devour – to eat up hungrily; to beat or destroy completely

balm – cream used for medicine, or anything that heals or soothes

profit – get a benefit, often refers to money

prosper – to succeed financially or physically

garment – a piece of clothing

supervise – to keep watch over someone while they work

confine – to place restrictions on someone or something

interpretation – the explanation of something's meaning

gaunt – scrawny looking, especially looking thin from hunger

subsequent – coming after something, following

discern – to be able to recognize or to see something and distinguish what it is

Vocabulary Review 9

Here are the clues to complete the crossword puzzle on the following page.

Across:

2. coming after something, following

5. to stay a short time in a place such as a home or hotel

8. the act of lying

10. the explanation of something's meaning

14. to place restrictions on someone or something

15. to win, to be widespread or more frequently occurring

16. to scold; to sharply tell someone their behavior is wrong

Down:

1. weak

3. to keep watch over someone while they work

4. scrawny looking, especially looking thin from hunger

6. a piece of clothing

7. to eat up hungrily; to beat or destroy completely

8. a large crowd

9. jealousy; being upset over what someone else has and you don't

11. word that describes how something is done

12. to be able to recognize or to see something and distinguish what it is

13. to succeed financially or physically

14. related to a subject (minus -ing)

15. get a benefit, often refers to money

17. cream used for medicine, or anything that heals or soothes

Need help? Look at the list on Vocabulary Review 8.

Science Review

Science Review 2

Circle the letter of the correct answer.

1. gills
A.   scales
B.   slits through which fish breathe
C.   organs
D.   animal homes

2. invertebrates
A.   animals with no backbones
B.   animals known for being followers
C.   animals that eat only plants
D.   animals with backbones

3. insects
A.   animals that are invertebrates, have antennae and exoskeletons and six legs
B.   animals that are warm-blooded, lay eggs, have two legs and feathers, vertebrates
C.   animals that eat only meat
D.   animals that are warm-blooded, give birth to live babies, vertebrates, have hair

4. herbivores
A.   used by insects for feeling and smelling
B.   animals that only eat meat
C.   animal homes
D.   animals that eat only plants

5. ecology
A.   animal homes
B.   animals that eat only plants
C.   the study of how living things live and interact together
D.   animals with no backbones

6. biome
A.   the broad characteristic of an animal habitat such as desert or mountain
B.   the study of how living things live and interact together
C.   used by insects for feeling and smelling
D.   animals that only eat plants

7. ecosystem
A.   slits through which fish breathe
B.   an area where living things live and interact together
C.   animals with backbones
D.   the study of living things and how the interact together

8. birds

A.   animals that are warm-blooded, give birth to live babies, vertebrates, have hair
B.   the study of how living things live and interact together
C.   animals that are warm-blooded, lay eggs, have two legs, have feathers, vertebrates
D.   animals that eat only meat

9. reptiles

A.   animals with no backbones
B.   an area where living things live and interact together
C.   animals that are cold-blooded, lay eggs, have scales, carnivores, vertebrates
D.   animals that eat only meat

10. sheep

A.   animals known for being followers
B.   animals known for their speed and agility
C.   animals that are vertebrates, lay eggs, have gills, have scales, cold-blooded
D.   animals that are cold-blooded, lay eggs, have scales, carnivores, vertebrates

11. vertebrates

A.   animals with no backbones
B.   animals that eat only plants
C.   animals with backbones
D.   used by insects for feeling and smelling

12. mammals

A.   animals that are warm-blooded, give birth to live babies, vertebrates, have hair
B.   animals that are invertebrates, have antennae and exoskeletons and six legs
C.   animals that are vertebrates, lay eggs, have gills, have scales, cold-blooded
D.   animals that are cold-blooded, lay eggs, have scales, carnivores, vertebrates

13. exoskeleton

A.   each living thing's role in its biome
B.   animals that are warm-blooded, lay eggs, have two legs, have feathers, vertebrates
C.   animals that are vertebrates, lay eggs, have gills, have scales, cold-blooded
D.   hard external shell

14. niche

A.   each living thing's role in its biome
B.   the study of how living things live and interact together
C.   animal homes
D.   used by insects for smelling and feeling

15. carnivores
A.   animals that are warm-blooded, lay eggs, have two legs, have feathers, vertebrates
B.   animals that eat only meat
C.   animals that eat only plants
D.   organize by similarities

16. habitats
A.   slits through which fish breathe
B.   each living thing's role in its biome
C.   animals that eat only meat
D.   animal homes

17. fish
A.   animals that are warm-blooded, give birth to live babies, vertebrates, have hair
B.   animals that are vertebrates, lay eggs, have gills, have scales, cold-blooded
C.   animals that are invertebrates, have antennae and exoskeletons and six legs
D.   animals that eat only plants

18. classify
A.   spend lots of money
B.   each living thing's role in its biome
C.   an area where living things live and interact together
D.   organize by similarities

19. antennae
A.   animals with no backbones
B.   animals known for being followers
C.   slits through which fish breathe
D.   used by insects for feeling and smelling

Science Review 4

EclipseCrossword.com

Across

6. where two bones connect
7. water vapor turning into water droplets
9. revolve around
10. the heart and lungs are examples of this
12. the force that pulls a smaller object toward a larger one (& us toward the earth)
13. atoms in combination
14. carries the blood back to the heart
17. main branches of the circulatory system, carry blood away from the heart
18. trees with leaves that change color and fall in cold weather
20. the early growth of a seed plant
21. name of a water molecule
23. the bending of light
24. the ability to work
25. a cold-weather area of little precipitation
26. rock used for carvings and engravings
27. rain and snow are examples of this

Down

1. main gas found in the air
2. an area of the world known for little precipitation
3. rocks orbiting a star
4. seeds being moved around
5. trees with needles that stay green all winter
8. the building blocks for all things
11. the layer of gases between earth and space
15. how high land is
16. unplanted
19. water turning into water vapor
22. largest bone in the body, thigh bone

Leave a space between words when the answer has more than one word in it. If you need help, the list of words is on Days 30 and 31.

Science Review 5
Circle the letter of the correct answer.

1. the heart and lungs are examples of this
A.   atoms   B.   refraction
C.   organs   D.   evaporation

2. largest bone in the body
A.   femur   B.   tibula
C.   molecule   D.   gravity

3. revolve around
A.   fallow   B.   cultivate
C.   femur   D.   orbit

4. an area of the world known for little precipitation
A.   biome   B.   desert
C.   mountain   D.   femur

5. metal used for tools and weapons
A.   bronze   B.   bdellium
C.   gold   D.   nitrogen

6. the layer of gases between earth and space
A.   condensation   B.   atmosphere
C.   precipitation   D.   gravity

7. the force that pulls a smaller object towards a larger one (& us down toward the earth)
A.   precipitation   B.   deciduous
C.   gravity   D.   arteries

8. trees with needles that stay green all winter
A.   deciduous   B.   femur
C.   coniferous   D.   dispersal

9. the early growth of a seed plant
A.   dispersal   B.   energy
C.   germination   D.   organ

10. atoms in combination
A.   vein   B.   refraction
C.   molecules   D.   joint

11. water vapor turning into water droplets
A.   evaporation   B.   desert
C.   condensation   D.   dispersal

12. seeds being moved around
A.   deciduous   B.   germination
C.   dispersal   D.   elevation

13. how high land is
A.   molecules   B.   dispersal
C.   elevation   D.   femur

14. the ability to work
A.   joint   B.   dispersal
C.   energy   D.   refraction

15. the bending of light
A.   germination   B.   refraction
C.   orbit   D.   reflection

16. rain and snow are examples of this
A.   precipitation   B.   tundra
C.   condensation   D.   elevation

17. water turning into water vapor
A.   evaporation   B.   precipitation
C.   condensation   D.   fallow

18. trees with leaves that change color and fall in cold weather
A.   coniferous   B.   deciduous
C.   germination   D.   dispersal

19. carry the blood back to the heart
A.   veins   B.   arteries
C.   solar system   D.   dispersal

20. the building blocks for all things
A.   coniferous   B.   refraction
C.   atoms   D.   organ

21. a cold-weather area of little precipitation
A.   dispersal   B.   desert
C.   atmosphere   D.   tundra

22. Air is mostly made up of which gas?
A.   oxygen   B.   molecules
C.   nitrogen   D.   organ

23. rocks orbiting a star
A.   germination   B.   solar system
C.   dispersal   D.   condensation

24. where two bones connect
A.   femur   B.   joint
C.   refraction   D.   nitrogen

25. the main branches of the circulatory system that carry blood away from the heart
A.   arteries   B.   veins
C.   elevation   D.   femur

26. unplanted
A.   fallow   B.   energy
C.   atoms   D.   atmosphere

Science Review 9

1. when something can go on forever
A.   evaporation
B.   sustainable
C.   bicep
D.   humidity

2. when a mixture separates over time
A.   involuntary muscles
B.   artesian wells
C.   suspension
D.   groundwater

3. type of cell in the brain
A.   delta
B.   neuron
C.   dispersion
D.   headwaters

4. slows the growth of microorganisms
A.   suspension
B.   density
C.   dispersion
D.   antiseptic

5. how much water is in the air
A.   humidity
B.   penicillin
C.   delta
D.   curds

6. a metal made by mixing other elements
A.   bicep
B.   antibiotic
C.   glucose
D.   alloy

7. where the river ends and the water fans out making a fertile area
A.   glucose
B.   channel
C.   delta
D.   microscopic

8. when water travels against gravity, climbing up whatever it is clinging to
A.   reflexes
B.   transpiration
C.   capillary action
D.   colloid

9. studies fossils
A.   saturated
B.   paleontologist
C.   suspension
D.   cells

10. chemical process where a molecule gains an oxygen atom
A.   fermentation
B.   evaporation
C.   oxidation
D.   tsunami

11. movements that our bodies do by instinct
A.   fermentation
B.   suspension
C.   cells
D.   reflexes

12. how much stuff is in a space
A.   paleontologist
B.   oxidation
C.   density
D.   humidity

13. bacteria killer
A.   delta
B.   saturated
C.   antibiotic
D.   dispersion

14. when light separates into colors
A.   ATP
B.   penicillin
C.   dispersion
D.   antiseptic

15. needs a microscope in order to be seen
A.   microscopic
B.   evaporation
C.   density
D.   humidity

16. the first antibiotic
A.   cells
B.   quicksand
C.   penicillin
D.   antibiotic

17. water in the ground
A.   dispersion
B.   density
C.   humidity
D.   groundwater

18. where water collects underground because it can't go any further because of saturation
A.   involuntary muscles
B.   density
C.   water table
D.   tributaries

19. a river that feeds into another river
A.   tributary
B.   oxidation
C.   antiseptic
D.   penicillin

20. when there's water over land where there isn't normally
A.   flood
B.   delta
C.   bicep
D.   microscopic

21. evaporation of the water from within plants
A.   dispersion
B.   water table
C.   transpiration
D.   calorie
Bonus: How do you think that's related to perspiration?

22. protein solids separated out from milk
A.   springs
B.   neurons
C.   curds
D.   contract

23. full
A.   paleontologist
B.   sustainable
C.   saturated
D.   delta

24. muscles that work without us controlling them
A.   bicep
B.   dispersion
C.   calorie
D.   involuntary muscles

25. sugar used by our bodies that it gets from our food
A.   simple machines
B.   glucose
C.   cells
D.   neurons

26. the big muscle that contracts when you bend your arm up at the elbow
A.   involuntary muscles
B.   antibiotic
C.   bicep
D.   glucose

27. a barrier that holds in heat
A.   bicep
B.   insulation
C.   antibiotic
D.   glucose

28. where our bodies store energy
A.   ATP
B.   tributaries
C.   glucose
D.   neurons

29. where a river begins
A.   headwaters
B.   cells
C.   meanders
D.   microscopic

30. a measurement of the energy found in food
A.   tributary
B.   calorie
C.   density
D.   evaporation

31. the body's building blocks
A.   cells
B.   contract
C.   reflexes
D.   paleontologist

32. when a mixture doesn't separate
A.   springs
B.   dispersion
C.   headwaters
D.   colloid

33. a huge tidal wave caused by an earthquake
A.   sustainable
B.   groundwater
C.   tsunami
D.   density

34. when a liquid becomes a gas
A.   penicillin
B.   evaporation
C.   neurons
D.   cells

Science Review 10

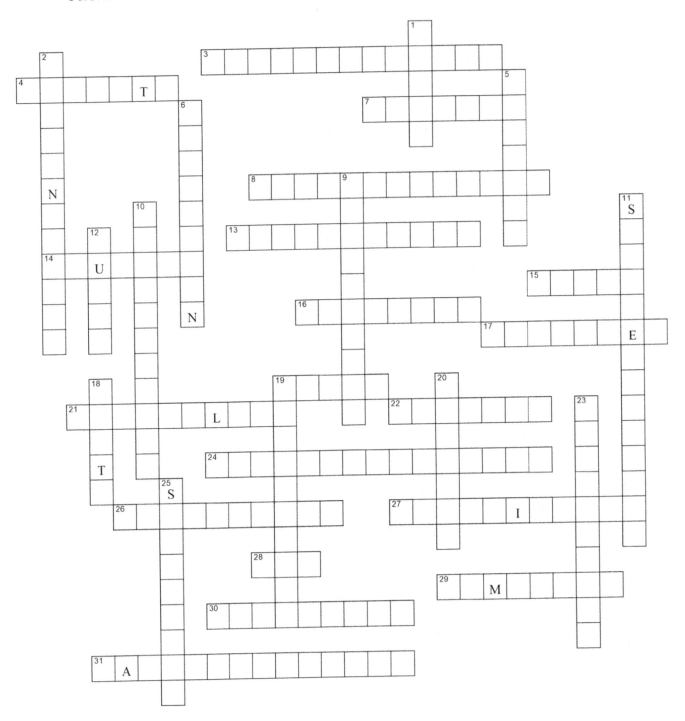

Science Review 10 Crossword Puzzle Clues

Across:

3. where water shoots up out of the ground
4. how much stuff is in a space
7. a measurement of the energy found in food
8. evaporation of the water from within plants
13. needs a microscope in order to be seen
14. a huge tidal wave caused by an earthquake
15. the big muscle that contracts when you bend your arm up at the elbow
16. how a muscle moves, stacking up muscle fiber bundles
17. movements that our bodies do by instinct
19. a metal made by mixing other elements
21. the first antibiotic
22. when a mixture doesn't separate
24. when water clings to something and travels up against gravity
26. where a river begins
27. something that can go on forever
28. where our bodies store energy
29. how much water is in the air
30. where sand is saturated with water and then some so that the sand starts floating
31. studies fossils

Down:

1. the body's building blocks
2. the chemical process that breaks down a substance
5. type of brain cells
6. chemical process where a molecule gains an oxygen atom
9. when a mixture separates over time
10. when a liquid becomes a gas
11. make work easier
12. protein solids separated out from milk
18. where the river ends and the water fans out making a fertile area
19. slows the growth of microorganisms
20. sugar used by our bodies that it gets from our food
23. bacteria killer
25. full

*Do not leave spaces between words when filling in the puzzle.

Words: saturated, cells, paleontologist, contract, density, antibiotic, fermentation, penicillin, water table, density, glucose, reflexes, neurons, humidity, calorie, antiseptic, oxidation, ATP, transpiration, alloy, delta, sustainable, suspension, microscopic, curds, evaporation, headwaters, tsunami, capillary action, bicep, simple machines, colloid

Science Review 11

Periodic Table

Chlorine
Here's a section of the periodic table. Use it to answer the following questions.

oxygen 8 O 15.999	fluorine 9 F 18.998	neon 10 Ne 20.180
sulfur 16 S 32.065	chlorine 17 Cl 35.453	argon 18 Ar 39.948

What is the symbol for chlorine? _____

What is the atomic number for chlorine? _____

What is the atomic mass for chlorine? _____

How many protons are in a chlorine atom? _____

How many electrons are in a chlorine atom? _____

About how many neutrons are in a chlorine atom? _____
(Hint: 17 + 17 = 34)

Draw a diagram of a chlorine atom.

Science Review 12

Circle one option from each set of choices. It's best to choose different options for each dog. After you make your choices, you can draw a picture of each if you like.

MOM DOG:
Hair: long or short
Body: big or small or medium
Legs: long or short
Ears: long or short
Coat: solid or spotted
Color: brown or white or black
Tail: long or short

DAD DOG:
Hair: long or short
Body: big or small or medium
Legs: long or short
Ears: long or short
Coat: solid or spotted
Color: brown or white or black
Tail: long or short

For each trait, circle either odd or even.

Hair: odd/even   Ears: odd/even   Body: odd/even   Tail: odd/even
Legs: odd/even   Coat: odd/even   Color: odd/even

Now, build your baby dog. Ask your parent to read you the rest of the instructions.

Hair: long or short
Body: big or small or medium
Legs: long or short
Ears: long or short
Coat: solid or spotted
Color: brown or white or black
Tail: long or short

Science Review 13

Element symbols: Oxygen: O   Carbon: C   Hydrogen: H   Sodium: Na

Look at this chemical equation. What do you recognize?
$NaHCO_3$ (baking soda) + $HC_2H_3O_2$ (vinegar) → $NaC_2H_3O_2$ + H_2O + CO_2

It's just sodium, carbon, hydrogen and oxygen atoms in different combinations.

What do we call atoms in combinations? _____

The chemical equation above says that baking soda added to vinegar will give you the stuff on the right. Do you recognize H_2O and CO_2?

What molecule is H_2O? _____

What does the 2 mean? _____

Can you remember or figure out what CO_2 stands for?
_____

Let's look at oxygen. Use the periodic table in the back of your workbook to answer the questions. Then draw an oxygen atom.

What is oxygen's atomic number? _____

How many protons does oxygen have? Where are they? _____

How many electrons does oxygen have? Where are they? _____

Oxygen's atomic mass is about 16. How many neutrons does oxygen have then? Where are they? _____

Science Review 14

Draw a double helix.

That's the structure of _____. It's found in our cells in long

strips called _____. There are _____

pairs of them in the _____ of our cells. The sections of them

are called _____. They are the _____

to the cells that make each of us unique. The genes, the instructions, are delivered by

the messenger, the _____. It's delivered to ribosomes who

follow the instructions to _____ a protein. The

_____ is the robot worker who just carries out the one job it

was built to do.

Word Box:
nucleus, protein, DNA, genes, chromosomes, RNA, instructions, twenty-three, build

---

Let's look at one trait. Let's look at noses. Let's say that there are two genes that determine the shape of your nose. (I don't know all that goes into it! We're just supposing here.) We're going to say that one gene determines the length of your nose: long or short. We're going to say that the second gene determines the shape of a nose: round or pointy.

You are going to roll a die. If it lands on an odd, then you write uppercase B. If it lands on an even number then write lowercase b.

Uppercase B stands for the dominant trait. If you get an at least one uppercase B, then the dominant gene is present and you have that trait.

Look at the following images of long and short noses. What type of nose shows the trait of the dominant gene? (Note: the short nose, has the capital B)

We're going to roll the die to determine what your grandparents' noses look like.

B

b

Roll for two Bs and write your results here: _____ _____. (grandfather)
Roll two more times and write the results here: _____ _____ . (grandmother)
If you have at least one B in a set of two blanks, then is the nose short or long? (Short because it's the dominant trait.)

B

b

Roll for two Bs an write your results here: _____ _____. (grandfather)
Roll two more times and write the results here: _____ _____ . (grandmother)
If you wrote two lowercase bs together, then is the nose round or pointy? (Pointy because the dominant trait, in this case round, is not present.)

Those results are your grandparents' genes. I know your grandparents on both sides aren't identical, but for the game they can be. Now let's find your parents' noses.

Using the letters you filled in the blanks with above, write your two results for long versus short noses. You'll write them on the boxes on the next page. One result goes on the top of the boxes, one on the side of the boxes. Then fill in the squares. You can look at my example.

Do the same thing for the round versus pointy.

Then fill in the possible combinations by writing the letter above and to the left of the box.

Now, roll a die until you get a number between 1 and 4 for mom. Write down the number. Then roll again for dad. Write down his number. Write the gene combination for the number square you rolled.

Here's an example:

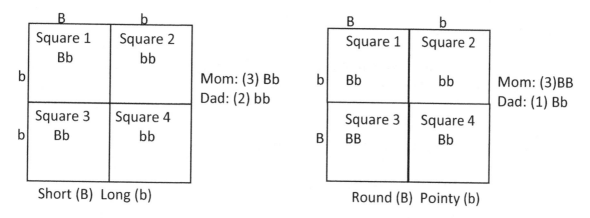

You use the boxes below:

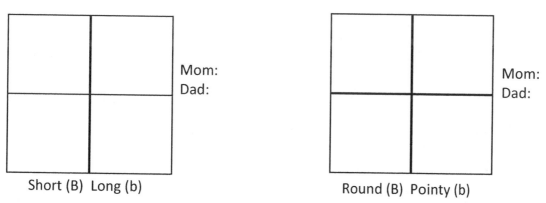

What does your mom's nose look like (in this activity)? What does your dad's look like? If the dominate gene is present, then the dominant trait is what you get. Now we get to find out what *your* nose is going to look like. Fill in the charts below as before with your mom's gene description on the top and your dad's gene description on the side. Write in the possibilities. Roll the die until you get a number between one and four. The gene description in that box is yours! What's your nose like? Want to draw a picture?

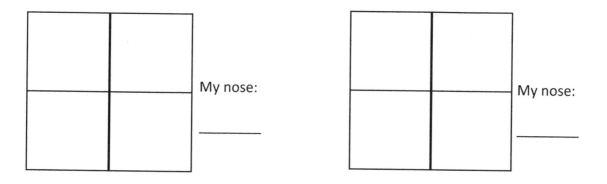

Science Review 15

Lesson 93 Metric Measures

10 millimeter = 1 centimeter; 100 centimeters = 1 meter; 1000 meters = 1 kilometer

Convert the measurements.

How far is 300 centimeters in meters? _____ meters
    Older kids, in millimeters and kilometers?

How far is 7 meters in centimeters? _____ centimeters
    Older kids, in millimeters and kilometers?

Explore more: Convert 1.75 meters and 1200 feet.

Label the parts of the eye (Day 71). The pupil is what opens to let in light. The retina is what receives the focused light to send the signals to the brain. The cornea is the part that refracts the light just right.

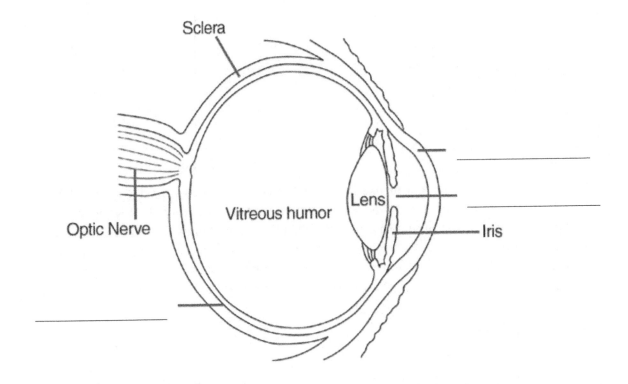

Science Review 15 continued

Match the terms and their definitions. Write the number of the definition that best matches in the blank provided.

_____ laughter

_____ nervous system

_____ immune system

_____ endorphins

_____ oxen

_____ saline

_____ glacier

_____ stalactite

_____ stalagmite

_____ prairie

_____ savannah

_____ stars

_____ combustion

_____ tinder

_____ scale balance

1. salt water

2. burning

3. balls of burning gas

4. African grasslands

5. large, floating ice formation

6. a spontaneous reaction causing muscle contraction

7. small, dry materials easily burned

8. body system that fights sickness

9. rock formation that hangs down

10. rock formation that pokes up from the ground

11. animal used for pulling loads

12. tool used for weighing

13. body system that sends signals to and from the brain

14. American grasslands

15. chemical that stops pain signals

Science Review 16

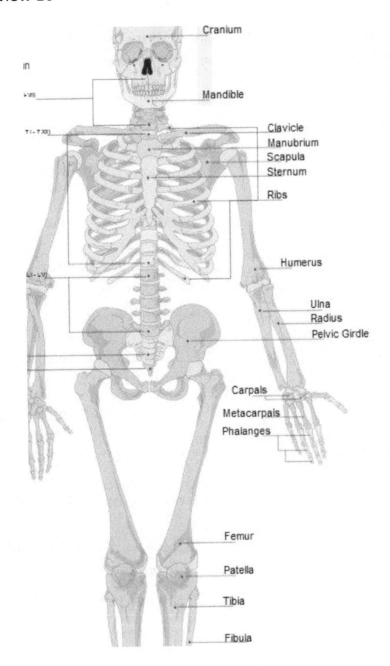

Science Review 17

Food Preservation Experiment

Question:
Are salting, dehydrating, and air tight packing effective preservation techniques?

Materials:

_____

_____

Procedure:

1. _____

2. _____

3. _____

4. _____

Observations:

1. _____

2. _____

3. _____

4. _____

Conclusion:

_____

_____

Science Review 18

Question:

_____

Materials:

_____

_____

Procedure:

1. _____

2. _____

3. _____

4. _____

Observations:

1. _____

2. _____

3. _____

4. _____

Conclusion:

_____

_____

Social Studies Review

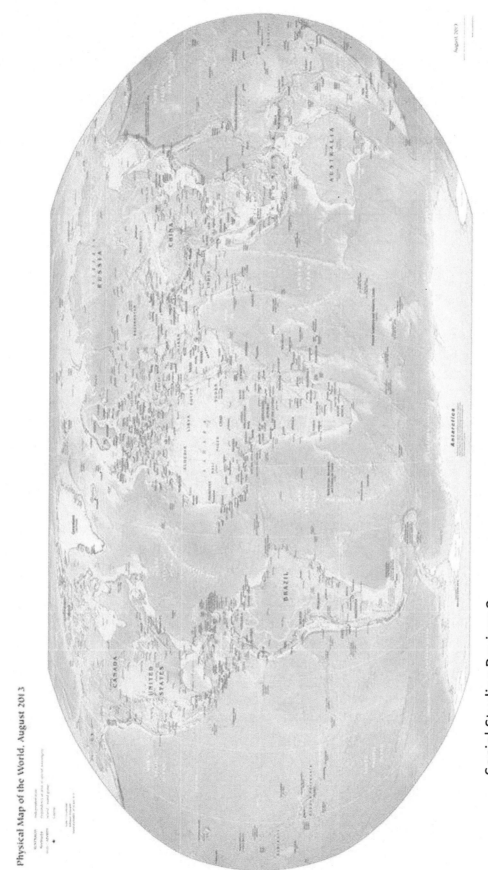

Physical Map of the World, August 2013

Social Studies Review 2

1. Label the continents and oceans.   2. Draw the equator and label the hemispheres.
3. Draw a symbol on your map and create a key to identify it.   4. Draw a constellation.

Social Studies Review 4

1. Where was the Fertile Crescent? Draw a boomerang around the area on the map.

2. Draw an X in the area where Mesopotamia was found.

3. Who would have lived in this area, a nomadic society or an agricultural society?

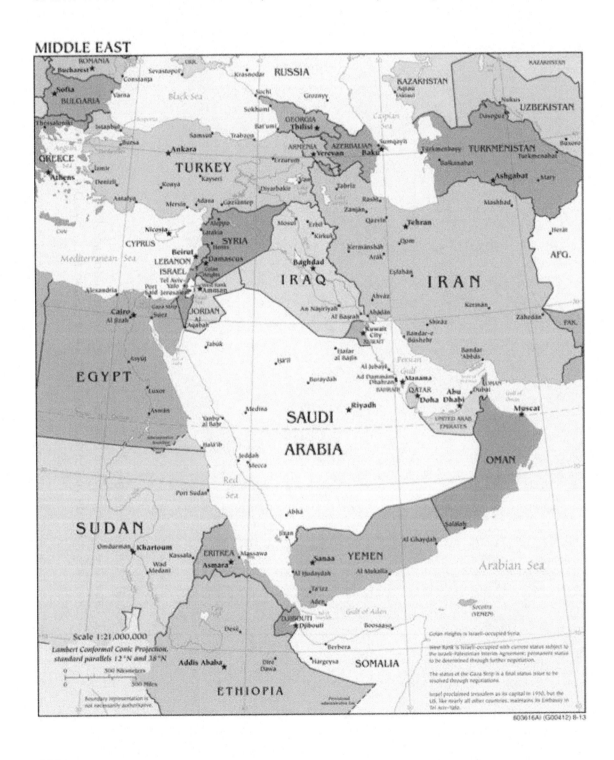

Social Studies Review 5

Abraham's Travels

Social Studies Review 7
Directions: Write the number in the blank of the matching item.

1. Abraham

2. Arabs

3. Babylon

4. boats in Mesopotamia

5. covenant

6. George Washington Carver

7. Hagar

8. Hammurabi

9. Hercules

10. hospitality

11. immigrants

12. Indo-European

13. Isaac

14. Lake Baikal

15. Mao Zedong

16. Melchizedek

17. The Great Lakes

18. The Greatest Generation

19. The Remnant

___A. king and priest, had communion with Abraham

___B. promise that can't be broken

___C. founder of the communist party in China

___D. largest language family

___E. enabled trade between cities

___F. fought in WWII

___G. botanist, someone who studies plants

___H. means he laughs

___I. These are a large portion of fresh surface water.

___J. wrote famous code of law

___K. descendants of Ishmael

___L. someone who comes to a new country to live

___M. those remaining in the faith

___N. famous for hanging gardens

___O. making people welcome in your home

___P. slave from Egypt and mother of Ishmael

___Q. largest fresh water lake, found in Russia

___R. strong man of Greek mythology

___S. means father of multitude

Social Studies Review 8
Match the letters (A – J) on the map to the place names.

_____ Tigris River   _____ Mediterranean Sea

_____ Egypt   _____ Euphrates River

_____ Red Sea   _____ Nile River

_____ Negev   _____ Israel/Canaan

_____ Ur/Babylon   _____ Mount Ararat
(Ur was down river from Babylon, but that's the general location of both)

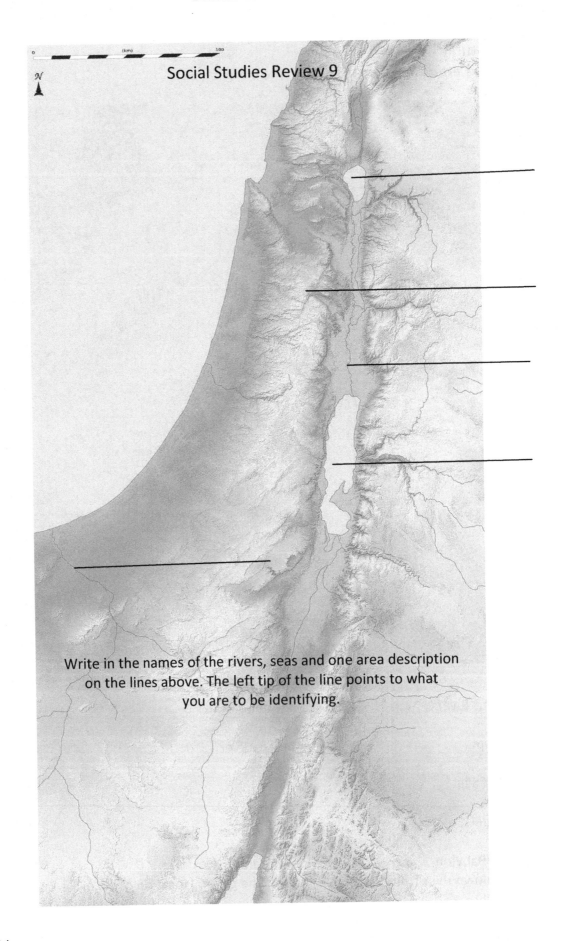

Social Studies Review 9

Write in the names of the rivers, seas and one area description on the lines above. The left tip of the line points to what you are to be identifying.

Social Studies Review 10

Name the countries of the Middle East. We've talked about numbers 1-5. Can you identify them without looking at a map? Use the Day 52 Middle East maps to help you complete the labeling. (Hint: number 9 isn't a country.)

Bonus: What are the names of the Palestinian areas carved out of Israel?

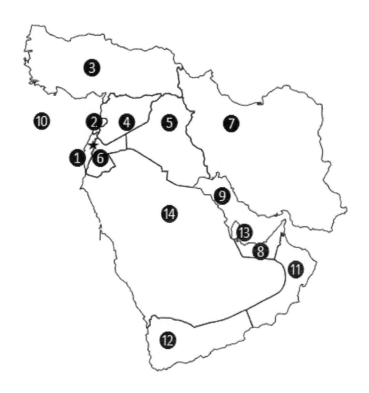

1. _____

2. _____

3. _____

4. _____

5. _____

6. _____

7. _____

8. _____

9. _____

10. _____

11. _____

12. _____

13. _____

14. _____

Bonus:

Social Studies Review 11

_____ Australia   _____ Canada   _____ Turkey   _____ Brazil   _____ India   _____ South Africa

_____ England   _____ Egypt   _____ USA   _____ Mexico   _____ France   _____ China

Social Studies Review 11 continued

Name these locations of the Middle East. (Hint: Numbers 9 and 10 aren't countries.)
Bonus: What are the names of the Palestinian areas carved out of Israel?

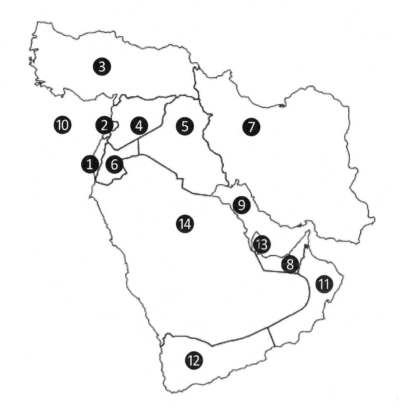

1. _____   2. _____

3. _____   4. _____

5. _____   ___ Mediterranean Sea

___ Persian Gulf   ___ United Arab Emirates

___ Yemen   ___ Qatar

___ Saudi Arabia   ___ Jordan

___ Oman   ___ Iran

Social Studies Review 11 Continued

_____ New Zealand   _____ Philippines   _____ Germany   _____ Cuba   _____ Chile   _____ Libya
_____ Russia   _____ Morocco   _____ Finland   _____ Peru   _____ Spain   _____ Thailand

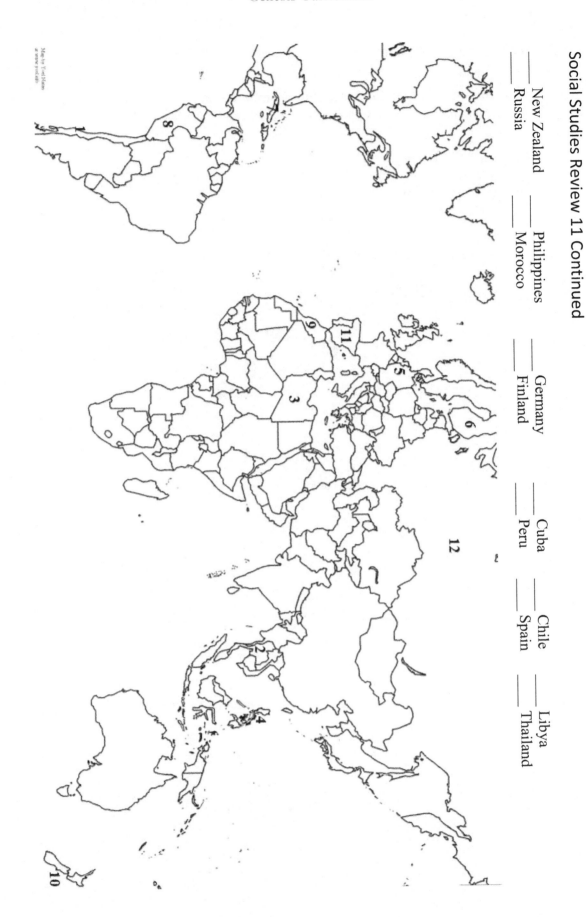

Social Studies Review 12

Social Studies Review 12
Statehood Date List

The original 13 colonies are already labeled on the map with when they became states.
Delaware was the first state to be *ratified*, which just means made official. The little
lines connect the smaller states to a state labeled with the year they were ratified.

Use this list to complete your assignments.
(Adapted from http://en.wikipedia.org/wiki/List_of_U.S._states_by_date_of_admission_to_the_Union)

14   Vermont   March 4, 1791
15   Kentucky   June 1, 1792
      Part of Virginia, seceded with the approval of the Virginia General Assembly
16   Tennessee   June 1, 1796
17   Ohio   March 1, 1803
18   Louisiana   April 30, 1812
19   Indiana   December 11, 1816
20   Mississippi   December 10, 1817
21   Illinois   December 3, 1818
22   Alabama   December 14, 1819
23   Maine   March 15, 1820
      Part of Massachusetts, seceded with the approval of the Mass. General Court
24   Missouri   August 10, 1821
25   Arkansas   June 15, 1836
26   Michigan   January 26, 1837
27   Florida   March 3, 1845
28   Texas   December 29, 1845
29   Iowa   December 28, 1846
30   Wisconsin   May 29, 1848
31   California   September 9, 1850
32   Minnesota   May 11, 1858
33   Oregon   February 14, 1859
34   Kansas   January 29, 1861
35   West Virginia June 20, 1863
      Part of Virginia, seceded with the approval of the pro-Union Virginia
      government, but without the approval of the Virginia government in rebellion
36   Nevada   October 31, 1864

37	Nebraska	1867	44	Wyoming	1890
38	Colorado	1876	45	Utah	1896
39	North Dakota	1889	46	Oklahoma	1907
40	South Dakota	1889	47	New Mexico	1912
41	Montana	1889	48	Arizona	1912
42	Washington	1889	49	Alaska	1959
43	Idaho	1890	50	Hawaii	1959

Social Studies Review 13

Match the country names and numbers.

_____ New Zealand	_____ England	_____ Brazil	_____ Australia	_____ Finland	_____ Egypt	_____ India
_____ China	_____ Philippines	_____ Germany	_____ Peru	_____ Mexico	_____ France	_____ USA
_____ Russia	_____ Morocco	_____ Turkey	_____ Japan	_____ Iran	_____ South Africa	

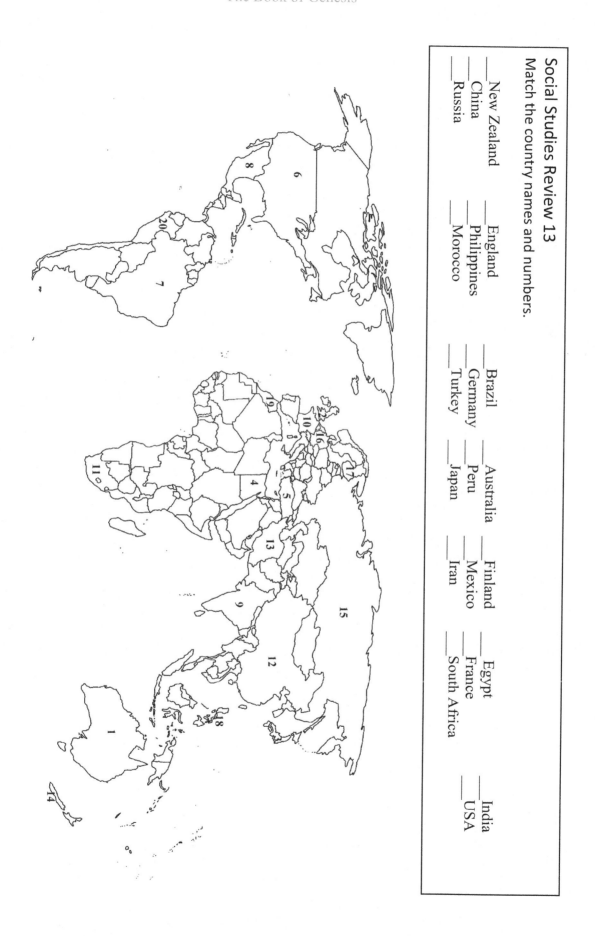

Social Studies Review 14
Spend. Save. Give.

Giving

Day #	Bank
	$100

131

132

133

134

135

136 Earn $50
New Total to Start:

Spending

End of the Day Bank:

137

138

139
Free Market:

Tax Amount:

Ending Bank Amount:

140

Final:

Social Studies Review 15

Who am I? Match the people to their descriptions. Write the correct name in the blank.

```
whistleblower                      Secretary of State
archeologist Howard Carter         George Müller
cryptologist                       Secretary of Energy
vizier                             George Washington Carver
slave                              Booker T. Washington
```

Social Studies Review 16

Read through the Bill of Rights overviews. Below are just the first five amendments to the Constitution. The Bill of Rights is the first ten amendments, or additions, to the US Constitution. The Bill of Rights was written shortly after the Constitution was written in 1787. The Constitution is the highest law of the land.

On Day 138 we'll do the second half of the Bill of Rights.

State which right, or rights, was violated in each case and which amendment gives that right.

First Amendment:
      1. government cannot establish a religion
      2. government cannot stop anyone from practicing their religion
      3. people have the right to peacefully protest
      4. people have the right to free speech

Second Amendment:
      1. people cannot be stopped from owning guns

Third Amendment:
      1. you can't be forced to let a soldier stay in your home

Fourth Amendment:
      1. your home cannot be searched without a warrant, which is special permission given only if there is good reason to search your home
      2. in the same way nothing can be taken from your home

Fifth Amendment:
      1. you can't be made to be a witness against yourself
      2. due process – you get to go through the justice system; you can't just be put in jail without having been accused and stand trial and be found guilty first
      3. you have to be told these basic rights

Case 1:
I published a newsletter about my dislike for the state flag, and the police called and told me to not say that ever again.

Amendment: _____

Right: _____

Case 2:
Police came and took away my computer and all of the copies of my newsletter without a warrant.

Amendment: _____

Right: _____

Case 3:
They took me into the prison and locked me up and never spoke to me.

Amendment: _____

Right: _____

Case 4:
My friends came to my defense and held up signs and chanted for my release, but they were forced to go home.

Amendment: _____

Right: _____

Case 5:
Make up a case to quiz your siblings and parents.

Social Studies Review 17

Read through the Bill of Rights overviews. Below are the next five amendments to the Constitution. The Bill of Rights is the first ten amendments, or additions, to the US Constitution. The Constitution was written in 1787 and the Bill of Rights was written shortly after. The Constitution is the highest law of the land.

State which right, or rights, was violated in each case and which amendment gives that right.

Sixth Amendment:
1. you have the right to a "speedy trial" (The rule now is that your trial has to happen within six months or you get to go free, unless it's a murder trial.)
2. you have the right to a jury among your peers who have to assume your innocence until there is proof of your guilt
3. you have the right to have an attorney, a lawyer, to speak for you at your trial

Seventh Amendment:
1. ensures a trial by jury in certain cases
2. the judge cannot override a decision made by the jury

Eighth Amendment:
1. you cannot be charged excessive fines as your punishment
2. you cannot be punished by cruel and unusual means

Ninth Amendment:
1. This says there are other rights that need to be protected.

Tenth Amendment:
1. any power not given to the government belongs to the states and the people

Case 1:
The president decides hoagies are the best sandwiches in the world and declares that the only sandwich that can be eaten is the hoagie.

Amendment: _____

Right:_____

Case 2:
You parked in an illegal parking space by mistake. The judge decides to never allow you to drive again and has your car taken away.

Amendment: _____

Right:_____

Case 3:
You are accused of not paying your dentist bills. You show up for your trial to find that all of the jurors are dentists. Instead of providing a lawyer for you, the judge says that the dentist accusing you will speak for you.

Amendment: _____

Right:_____

Case 4:
You are found innocent by the jury. The judge decides that they were wrong and sends you to prison.

Amendment: _____

Right:_____

Case 5:
Make up a case to quiz your siblings and parents.

Social Studies Review 18

This is kind of just for fun. In WWII cryptographers decoded messages sent by the Japanese. Below is a sentence you memorized this year. Each number stands for one letter, so if you figure out one word, use each number to fill in that same letter in all of the matching numbered spaces. (The first two lines have three words, and the last two lines each have two words.)

___ ___ ___ ___ ___ ___ ___ ___ ___ ___ ___ ___ ___ ___
 8   2   3   5   22   24   22   13   8   2   2   8   2   13

___ ___ ___ ___ ___ ___ ___ ___ ___ ___ ___ ___ ___
13   15   11   12   21   22   14   3   22   11   3   5   22

___ ___ ___ ___ ___ ___ ___ ___ ___ ___
 5   22   14   1   22   2   19   14   2   11

___ ___ ___ ___ ___ ___ ___ ___ .
 3   5   22   22   14   21   3   5

Social Studies Review 19
Timeline

3966   Creation (1...)
       Mesopotamia, Cradle of Civilization (14)
2910   Noah (41)
2310   flood (40)
2200   Tower of Babel (46)
       Sumerians (95)
       Egyptian kingdoms begin during this time (121-122)
2018   Abraham born (47)

1990   Pyramids first appear (121)
1950   Sumerians attacked by the Elamites and Amorites (the beginning of the decline
       of the Sumerians) (95)
1918   Isaac born (79)
1750   Hammurabi, king of the Amorites, writes code of law (56)
600   Nebechadnezzer and the hanging gardens (60)
114   *Silk Road begins forming (92)
1   Jesus is born
70   *Jerusalem destroyed (from the section of fulfilled prophecies-58)

700   Silk Road trade at its peak (92)
1050   First spinning wheel invented (87 science)
1400   Decline of the Silk Road (92)
1500s Henry the 8th (famous for executing people) (76)
1621   *The First Thanksgiving (78)
1750- The Guinness family in Ireland is influenced by John Wesley (122)
1750   The beginning of the Industrial Revolution (87)

***From here on, all years are exact dates.
1777   October - all thirteen of the original American colonies celebrated a Thanksgiving
       feast (78)
1787   US Constitution written, acceptance by all of the states by 1790 (124)
1789   George Washington had the last Thursday of November of 1789 as a day of
       prayer and thanksgiving (78)
1791   Bill of Rights become official
1793 - 1794 The Reign of Terror was from September 1793 to July 1794. This was the
       beginning of the French Revolution and was marked by mass executions. (76)
1803   Louisiana Purchase (77)
1804   Lewis and Clark sent to explore the US (77)

1820- New technology was rapidly expanding the number of factories in Lowell Massachusetts during the 1820s and 30s (101)

1836 The first wagon trains leave on the Oregon Trail (77)

1845 Lowell Mill Girls form the first woman's union to protest their treatment (87)

1850- Gregor Mendel researched genetics in the second half of the 19th century. (89 science)

Put on when your state gained its statehood

1863 Emancipation Proclamation, an executive order issued on January 1, 1863, freed the slaves (103)

1863 Abraham Lincoln declares Thanksgiving a holiday (78)

1861 April 12, 1861 – April 9, 1865 The American Civil War (78, 103)

1891 George Washington Carver is the first black student at Iowa State Agricultural College. (110)

1920s Boll weevil devastates cotton crops and the economy of the southern states (48)

1922 King Tut's tomb discovered (121)

1924 Eric Liddell refuses to run on Sunday and ends up winning gold in the 100-meter race he hadn't trained for (12)

1928 Penicillin, the first antibiotic, was discovered in London by Alexander Fleming (56 science)

1930s Famine in Ukraine caused by the Soviet communists who controlled them (128)

1931 The Empire State Building in New York City opened (lesson on steel) (46 science)

1939 President Franklin moves Thanksgiving and confuses everyone (78)

1940 Penicillin becomes widespread in use (56 science)

1941 Congress passed into law that the fourth Thursday of November be declared Thanksgiving. (78)

WWII America and Japan (82, 104)

1941 December 7, 1941, Pearl Harbor was attacked

1942 April 18, 1942 Doolittle Raiders retaliate and attack Japan

1942 June 4-7 Battle of Midway, US defeats Japan by decoded their attack plans

1945 August 6, 1945, atomic bomb dropped on Hiroshima

1945 August 9, atomic bomb dropped on Nagasaki and Japan surrenders

1948 The nation of Israel is reinstated (from lesson on fulfilled prophecies-58)

1949 Mao Zedong becomes the communist leader of China and causes a horrific famine with his "Great Leap Forward."

1950 Dead Sea scrolls (ancient copies of the Bible) were found showing the Bible hadn't been changed over time (21)

1980s Ethiopian famine caused by communist tactics (128)

1991 Ukraine became its own country, separated from soviet Russia (128)

2000 - 2020 generation Z (37)

2005 Hurricane Katrina (39)

2011 Tsunami in Japan (39)

Hebrew
Writing

Hebrew Writing 1

You read Hebrew from right to left! Start with the Aleph on the top right and trace that one first. Then move to the one to its left. When you get to the end of the row, go back to the bottom right and trace that letter. That's how you write Hebrew. Remember, it's not backwards to them!

Trace Letter Aleph!

Silent Letter
takes the sound of its vowel

Trace the letter outline:

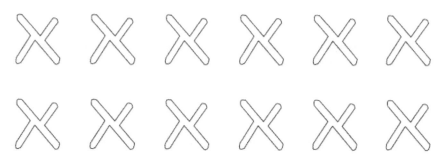

Genesis 1:3

וַיֹּאמֶר אֱלֹהִים, יְהִי אוֹר; וַיְהִי אוֹר.

Hebrew Writing 2

The Aleph (ah – lef) is the first letter of the Hebrew alphabet, but it doesn't make a sound! Remember to start on the right!

_____

_____

_____

_____

Genesis 1:5

וַיִּקְרָא אֱלֹהִים לָאוֹר יוֹם, וְלַחֹשֶׁךְ קָרָא לָיְלָה; וַיְהִי עֶרֶב וַיְהִי בֹקֶר, יוֹם אֶחָד.

Hebrew Writing 3

Remember: You read Hebrew from right to left. Start with the Bet on the top right and trace that one first. Then move to the one on its left. When you get to the end of the row, go back to the bottom right and trace that letter. That's how you write Hebrew. Remember, that to them, you are the one who writes backwards.

Trace Letter Bet!

"b" as in <u>b</u>oy
no dot – "v" as in <u>v</u>ine

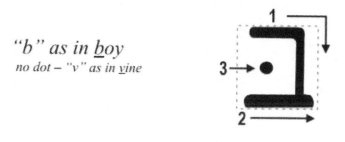

Trace the letter outline:

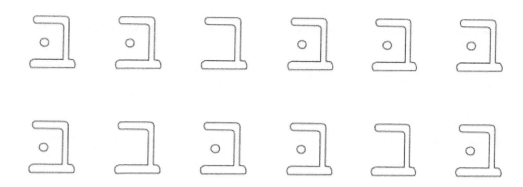

Genesis 1:1

בְּרֵאשִׁית, בָּרָא אֱלֹהִים, אֵת הַשָּׁמַיִם, וְאֵת הָאָרֶץ.

Hebrew Writing 4

The Bet can sound like B or V depending on whether or not it has a dot. Trace and write the letter Bet. As before, if you want to practice calligraphy, use the top line. Everyone should trace the bottom line and then write your own on the lines.

Genesis 1:5

וַיִּקְרָא אֱלֹהִים לָאוֹר יוֹם, וְלַחֹשֶׁךְ קָרָא לָיְלָה; וַיְהִי עֶרֶב וַיְהִי בֹקֶר, יוֹם אֶחָד.

Hebrew Writing 5

You read Hebrew from right to left! Remember to start with the Gimmel on the top right and trace that one first. Then move to the one to its left. When you get to the end of the row, go back to the bottom right and trace that letter. That's how you write Hebrew.

Trace Letter Gimmel!

"g" as in girl

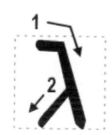

Trace the letter outline:

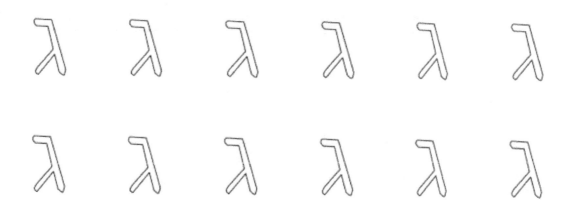

טז וַיַּעַשׂ אֱלֹהִים, אֶת-שְׁנֵי הַמְּאֹרֹת הַגְּדֹלִים:
אֶת-הַמָּאוֹר הַגָּדֹל, לְמֶמְשֶׁלֶת הַיּוֹם, וְאֶת-הַמָּאוֹר הַקָּטֹן
לְמֶמְשֶׁלֶת הַלַּיְלָה, וְאֵת הַכּוֹכָבִים.

Hebrew Writing 6

Trace and write Gimmel. The top line is for calligraphy.

Hebrew Writing 7

Trace and write the letters Aleph, Bet, Gimmel. I used a different font this time to show you the letters with a thinner line.

א   א   א   א   א

בּ   בּ   בּ   בּ   בּ

ג   ג   ג   ג   ג

א

_____

בּ

_____

ג

_____

Genesis Curriculum

Hebrew Writing 8

Remember to work from right to left. Start with the Dalet on the top right and trace that one first. Then move to the one to its left. When you get to the end of the row, go back to the bottom right and trace that letter. That's how you write Hebrew.

Trace Letter Dalet!

*"d" as in **door***

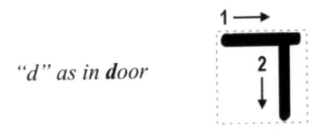

Trace the letter outline:

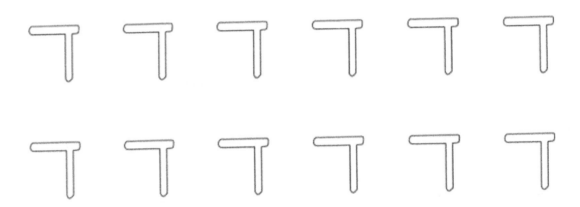

וַיַּרְא אֱלֹהִים אֶת הָאוֹר, כִּי טוֹב; וַיַּבְדֵּל אֱלֹהִים, בֵּין הָאוֹר וּבֵין הַחֹשֶׁךְ.
Genesis 1:4

וַיִּקְרָא אֱלֹהִים לָאוֹר יוֹם, וְלַחֹשֶׁךְ קָרָא לָיְלָה; וַיְהִי עֶרֶב וַיְהִי בֹקֶר, יוֹם אֶחָד.
Genesis 1:5

Hebrew Writing 9

The first line is for calligraphy. Trace the second line of the letter Dalet and then write your own.

Hebrew Writing 10

Here are the three words that have been introduced for letter practice.

devar: word, goel: kinsman redeemer, abba: father

The top half of the page is for calligraphy. The bottom half is print.

****

Hebrew Writing 11

Remember to work from right to left. Start with the Hei (Hey) on the top right and trace that one first. Then move to the one to its left. When you get to the end of the row, go back to the bottom right and trace that letter.

Trace Letter Hey!

"h" as in hay

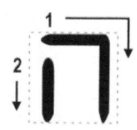

Trace the letter outline:

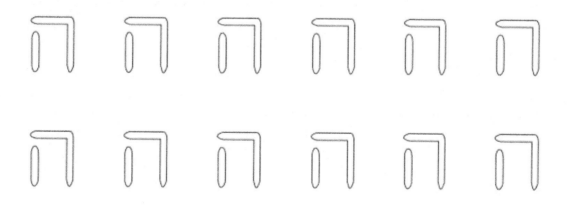

Genesis 1:2-3

ב וְהָאָרֶץ, הָיְתָה תֹהוּ וָבֹהוּ, וְחֹשֶׁךְ, עַל-פְּנֵי תְהוֹם ; וְרוּחַ אֱלֹהִים, מְרַחֶפֶת עַל-פְּנֵי הַמָּיִם.

ג וַיֹּאמֶר אֱלֹהִים, יְהִי אוֹר ; וַיְהִי-אוֹר.

Note: The bold letters that are separate at the beginning of each verse are the verse numbers in Hebrew. Do they look familiar? What letter do you think is the symbol for 1?

155

Hebrew Writing 12

The first line is for calligraphy. Trace the second line of the letter Hei and then write your own.

Hebrew Writing 13

Find all of the letters you have learned so far: Aleph, Bet, Gimmel, Dalet, Hei in Genesis 1:1-5. The bold separate letters at the beginning of each verse are the verse numbers. What do you notice about them?

א בְּרֵאשִׁית, בָּרָא אֱלֹהִים, אֵת הַשָּׁמַיִם, וְאֵת הָאָרֶץ.

ב וְהָאָרֶץ, הָיְתָה תֹהוּ וָבֹהוּ, וְחֹשֶׁךְ, עַל פְּנֵי תְהוֹם; וְרוּחַ אֱלֹהִים, מְרַחֶפֶת עַל פְּנֵי הַמָּיִם.

ג וַיֹּאמֶר אֱלֹהִים, יְהִי אוֹר; וַיְהִי אוֹר.

ד וַיַּרְא אֱלֹהִים אֶת הָאוֹר, כִּי טוֹב; וַיַּבְדֵּל אֱלֹהִים, בֵּין הָאוֹר וּבֵין הַחֹשֶׁךְ.

ה וַיִּקְרָא אֱלֹהִים לָאוֹר יוֹם, וְלַחֹשֶׁךְ קָרָא לָיְלָה; וַיְהִי עֶרֶב וַיְהִי בֹקֶר, יוֹם אֶחָד.

ה ד ג ב ב א

Be careful with ד. It's the very last letter in these verses.
Similar letters are not the same letter.

Hebrew Writing 14

Remember to work from right to left. Start with the Resh on the top right and trace within the lines of that one first. Then move to the one to its left. When you get to the end of the row, go back to the bottom right and trace that letter.

Trace Letter Resh!

"R" as in rain

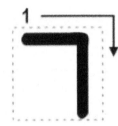

Trace the letter outline:

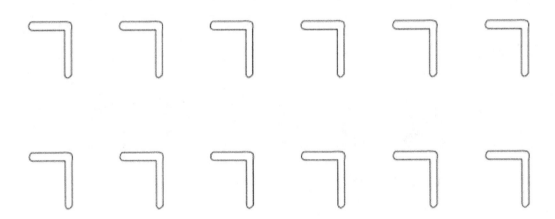

Genesis 1:1

בְּרֵאשִׁית, בָּרָא אֱלֹהִים, אֵת הַשָּׁמַיִם, וְאֵת הָאָרֶץ.

Hebrew Writing 15

The first line is for calligraphy. Trace the second line of the letter Resh and then write your own.

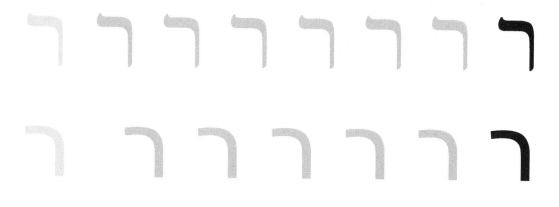

Hebrew Writing 16

Here are the three words: devar-word, goel-kinsman redeemer, bara-created.

Remember to read and write from right to left!
The top half of the page is for calligraphy. The bottom half is print.

Hebrew Writing 17

Remember to work from right to left.

Trace Letter Lamed!

"L" as in look

Trace the letter outline:

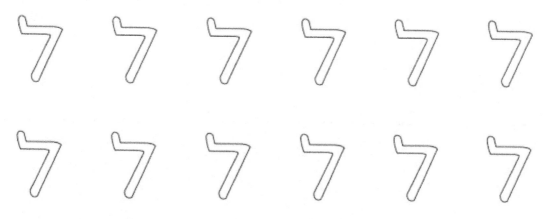

א בְּרֵאשִׁית, בָּרָא אֱלֹהִים, אֵת הַשָּׁמַיִם, וְאֵת הָאָרֶץ.

ב וְהָאָרֶץ, הָיְתָה תֹהוּ וָבֹהוּ, וְחֹשֶׁךְ, עַל פְּנֵי תְהוֹם; וְרוּחַ אֱלֹהִים, מְרַחֶפֶת עַל פְּנֵי הַמָּיִם.

ג וַיֹּאמֶר אֱלֹהִים, יְהִי אוֹר; וַיְהִי אוֹר.

ד וַיַּרְא אֱלֹהִים אֶת הָאוֹר, כִּי טוֹב; וַיַּבְדֵּל אֱלֹהִים, בֵּין הָאוֹר וּבֵין הַחֹשֶׁךְ.

ה וַיִּקְרָא אֱלֹהִים לָאוֹר יוֹם, וְלַחֹשֶׁךְ קָרָא לָיְלָה; וַיְהִי עֶרֶב וַיְהִי בֹקֶר, יוֹם אֶחָד.

161

Hebrew Writing 18

The first line is for calligraphy. Trace the second line of the letter Lamed and then write your own.

Hebrew Writing 19

Here are the three words: bara-created, eloheem-God, liila-night. There are two new letters in here. The apostrophe looking thing is a letter. Don't worry about that today. It's easy to figure out the sound of the last letter in eloheem.

Remember to read and write from right to left!
The top half of the page is for calligraphy. The bottom half is print.

****

Hebrew Writing 20

Remember to work from right to left. Start with the Vav on the top right and trace that one first. Then move to the one to its left. When you get to the end of the row, go back to the bottom right and trace that letter.

Trace Letter Vav!

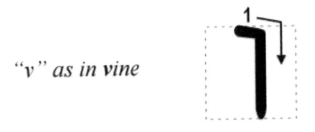

"v" as in vine

Trace the letter outline:

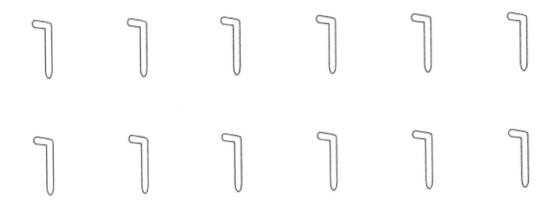

Genesis 1:1

בְּרֵאשִׁית, בָּרָא אֱלֹהִים, אֵת הַשָּׁמַיִם, וְאֵת הָאָרֶץ.

Hebrew Writing 21

The first line is for calligraphy. Trace the second line of the letter Vav and then write your own.

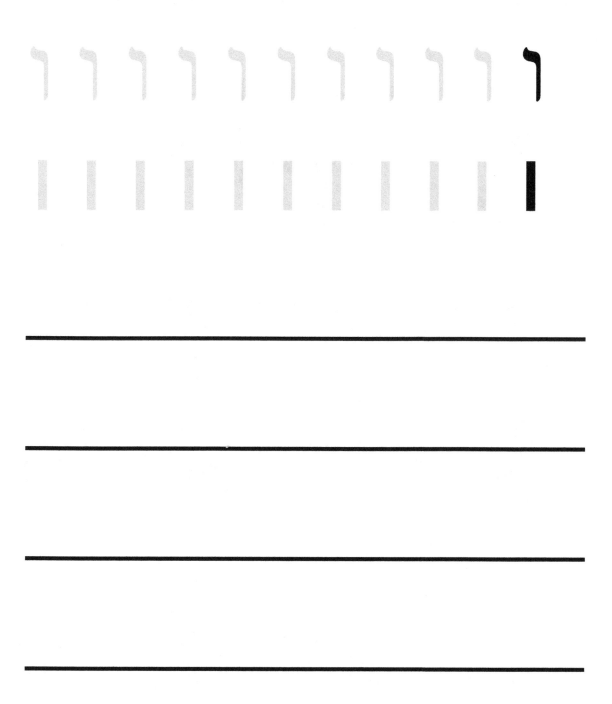

Hebrew Writing 22

Remember to work from right to left. Start with the Tav on the top right and trace that one first. Then move to the one to its left. When you get to the end of the row, go back to the bottom right and trace that letter.

Trace Letter Tav!

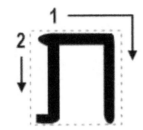

"T" as in tall
(with dot, same sound)

Trace the letter outline:

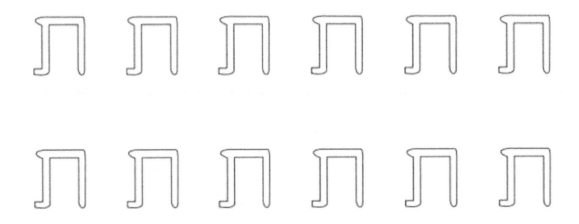

Genesis 1:1

בְּרֵאשִׁית, בָּרָא אֱלֹהִים, אֵת הַשָּׁמַיִם, וְאֵת הָאָרֶץ.

Hebrew Writing 23

The first line is for calligraphy. Trace the second line of the letter Tav and then write your own.

Hebrew Writing 24

Here are two words from last week: bara-created and eloheem-God. I've also added in VE ET (from Genesis 1:1). The VE only has one letter, the Vav. It connects to the ET after it to be written as one word. Since ET starts with a vowel, it begins the with Aleph.

Remember to read and write from right to left!
The top half of the page is for calligraphy. The bottom half is print.

****

Hebrew Writing 25

Remember to work from right to left. Start with the Yod on the top right and trace that one first. Then move to the one to its left. When you get to the end of the row, go back to the bottom right and trace that letter.

Trace Letter Yod!

"*Y*" *as in yes*

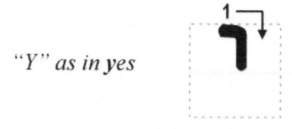

Trace the letter outline:

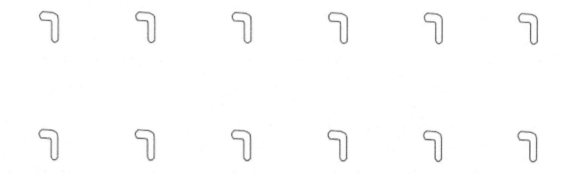

Genesis 1:1

בְּרֵאשִׁית, בָּרָא אֱלֹהִים, אֵת הַשָּׁמַיִם, וְאֵת הָאָרֶץ.

Hebrew Writing 26

The first line is for calligraphy. Trace the second line of the letter Yod and then write your own. I added another set with the letter in another font, so it's not just a straight line. I also added the line to show you that this letter is like an apostrophe; it hangs in the air and doesn't touch the line.

Hebrew Writing 27

Remember to work from right to left. Start with the Mem on the top right and trace that one first. Then move to the one to its left. When you get to the end of the row, go back to the bottom right and trace that letter.

Trace Letter Mem!

*"M" as in **mom***

Trace the letter outline:

Genesis 1:1

בְּרֵאשִׁית, בָּרָא אֱלֹהִים, אֵת הַשָּׁמַיִם, וְאֵת הָאָרֶץ.

Hebrew Writing 28

The first line is for calligraphy. Trace the second line of the letter Mem and then write your own. The line further down is the form of Mem that comes at the end of the word.

Hebrew Writing 29

Here are two words from last week: eloHEEM-God and ve et (from Genesis 1:1). The VE only has one letter, the Vav. It connects to the ET after it to be written as one word. The new word is shaMAyim, heavens. It has a new letter. We'll learn that next.

Remember to read and write from right to left!
The top half of the page is for calligraphy. The bottom half is print.

****

Hebrew Writing 30

Remember to work from right to left. Start with the Shin on the top right and trace that one first. Then move to the one to its left. When you get to the end of the row, go back to the bottom right and trace that letter.

Trace Letter Shin!

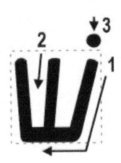

"Sh" as in shy
(dot left – "s" as in sun)

Trace the letter outline:

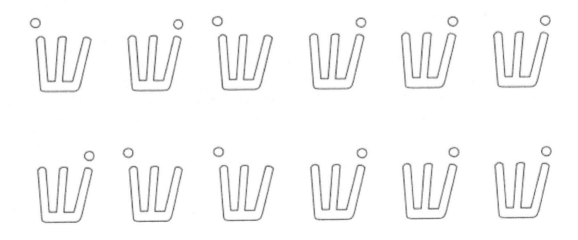

Genesis 1:1

בְּרֵאשִׁית, בָּרָא אֱלֹהִים, אֵת הַשָּׁמַיִם, וְאֵת הָאָרֶץ.

Can you find any words in here? You've written a few of them.

Hebrew Writing 31

The first line is for calligraphy. Trace the second line of the letter Shin and then write your own.

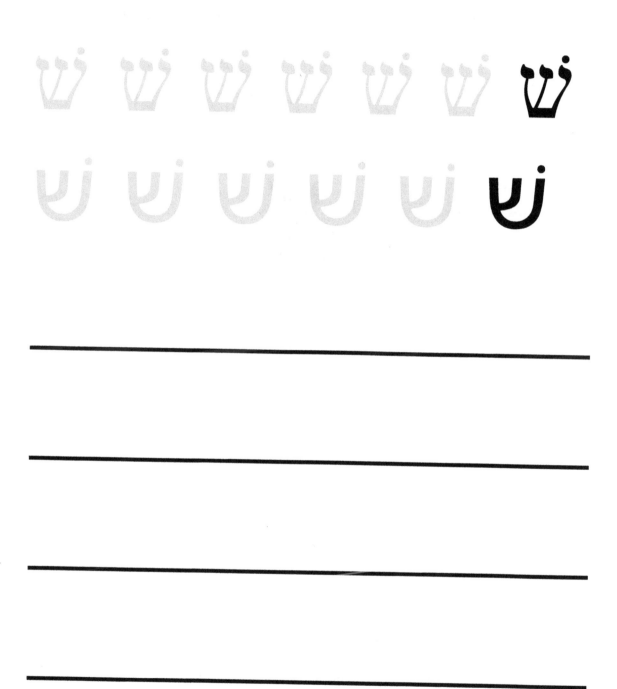

Hebrew Writing 32

Remember to work from right to left. Start with the Tsade on the top right and trace that one first. Then move to the one to its left. When you get to the end of the row, go back to the bottom right and trace that letter.

Trace Letter Tsade!

"Ts" as in nuts

Trace the letter outline:

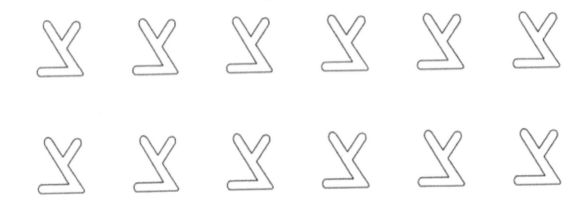

Genesis 1:1

בְּרֵאשִׁית, בָּרָא אֱלֹהִים, אֵת הַשָּׁמַיִם, וְאֵת הָאָרֶץ.

Where in here do you see the Shin and the Tsade?

Hebrew Writing 33

The first line is for calligraphy. Trace the second line of the letter Tsade and then write your own. At the bottom of the page is the form used only when the Tsade comes at the end of the word. A little part of the end form hangs down below the line, though it starts just as high as the other letters. You can see it in the last word of Genesis 1:1 on the Hebrew Writing 32 page.

Hebrew Writing 34

Today you are going to write Genesis 1:1! Remember to read and write from right to left!

Genesis 1:1

בְּרֵאשִׁית, בָּרָא אֱלֹהִים, אֵת הַשָּׁמַיִם, וְאֵת הָאָרֶץ.

בְּרֵאשִׁית, בָּרָא

אֱלֹהִים, אֵת

הַשָּׁמַיִם, וְאֵת

הָאָרֶץ.

בְּרֵאשִׁית, בָּרָא אֱלֹהִים, אֵת הַשָּׁמַיִם, וְאֵת הָאָרֶץ.

Hebrew Writing 35

Today you are going to write Genesis 1:3! Remember to read and write from right to left! You'll notice the word OR is written with three letters. The Vav is helping with the vowel sound in the word.

Genesis 1:3

וַיֹּאמֶר אֱלֹהִים, יְהִי אוֹר; וַיְהִי אוֹר.

va YOmer eloHEEM yeHEE or va yeHEE or

ויאמר אלהים יהי אור

יהי אור

ויאמר אלהים יהי אור

ויהי אור

Hebrew Writing 36

Remember to work from right to left. Start with the Ayin on the top right and trace that one first. Then move to the one to its left. When you get to the end of the row, go back to the bottom right and trace that letter.

Trace Letter Ayin!

Silent letter
takes the sound of its vowel

Trace the letter outline:

Genesis 1:2

וְהָאָרֶץ, הָיְתָה תֹהוּ וָבֹהוּ, וְחֹשֶׁךְ, עַל פְּנֵי תְהוֹם; וְרוּחַ
אֱלֹהִים, מְרַחֶפֶת עַל פְּנֵי הַמָּיִם.

Where do you see the Ayin?

Hebrew Writing 37

The first line is for calligraphy. Trace the second line of the letter Ayin and then write your own.

ע ע ע ע ע ע ע ע ע ע

ע ע ע ע ע ע ע ע ע

_____

_____

_____

_____

Hebrew Writing 38

Remember to work from right to left. Start with the Pey on the top right and trace that one first. Then move to the one to its left. When you get to the end of the row, go back to the bottom right and trace that letter.

Trace Letter Pey!

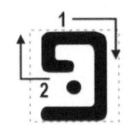

"P" as in park
no dot – "ph" as in phone

Trace the letter outline:

Genesis 1:2

Where do you see the Pey?

Hebrew Writing 39

The first line is for calligraphy. Trace the second line of the letter Pey and then write your own.

Hebrew Writing 40

Remember to work from right to left. Start with the Nun on the top right and trace that one first. Then move to the one to its left. When you get to the end of the row, go back to the bottom right and trace that letter.

Trace Letter Nun!

"N" as in now

נ

Trace the letter outline:

נ נ נ נ נ נ

נ נ נ נ נ נ

Genesis 1:2

וְהָאָרֶץ, הָיְתָה תֹהוּ וָבֹהוּ, וְחֹשֶׁךְ, עַל פְּנֵי תְהוֹם; וְרוּחַ
אֱלֹהִים, מְרַחֶפֶת עַל פְּנֵי הַמָּיִם.

Where do you see the Nun?

Hebrew Writing 41

The first line is for calligraphy. Trace the second line of the letter Nun and then write your own. At the bottom of the page is the end form of the letter Nun. That's what it looks like at the end of a word. It hangs down below the line a little bit, but it starts at the same height as the other letters.

Hebrew Writing 42

Trace and write al pnaa teHOM from Genesis 1:2.

וְהָאָרֶץ, הָיְתָה תֹהוּ וָבֹהוּ, וְחֹשֶׁךְ, עַל פְּנֵי תְהוֹם ; וְרוּחַ
אֱלֹהִים, מְרַחֶפֶת עַל פְּנֵי הַמָּיִם.

Remember to read and write from right to left! The Vav is taking on the O sound here. The top half of the page is for calligraphy. The bottom half is print.

עַל פְּנֵי תְהוֹם

עַל פְּנֵי תְהוֹם

עַל פְּנֵי תְהוֹם

Make sure you read the words. Don't just copy them.

Hebrew Writing 43

Remember to work from right to left. Start with the Chet and Khaf on the top right and trace that one first. Then move to the one to its left. When you get to the end of the row, go back to the bottom right and trace that letter.

Trace Letter Chet!

"ch" as in bach

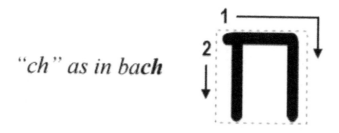

Trace the letter outline:

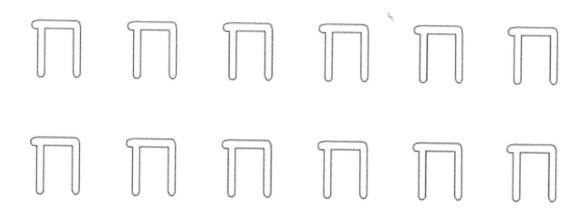

And the Khaf (below) is also transliterated in our Hebrew as KH. This is the end form of the letter. This is how you'll see it in our verses.

Hebrew Writing 44

The first line is for calligraphy. Trace the second line of the letter Chet and then write your own. Then write the Khaf. These are both found in the word KHOshekh. You'll see that the Khaf also hangs down low.

Hebrew Writing 45

Today you are going to trace, write, and read the first part of Genesis 1:2. Remember to read and write from right to left! The part we are doing today is the underlined part of the Hebrew and the transliterated part that's big and bold. Remember the Vav with a dot tucked into it makes the long U sound!

Genesis 1:2

וְהָאָרֶץ, הָיְתָה תֹהוּ וָבֹהוּ, וְחֹשֶׁךְ, עַל פְּנֵי תְהוֹם; וְרוּחַ אֱלֹהִים, מְרַחֶפֶת עַל פְּנֵי הַמָּיִם.

vehaArets haaTAH TOhu vaVOhu veKHOshekh al pnaa teHOM veRUakh eloHEEM meraKHEfet al pnaa haMAyim

וְהָאָרֶץ, הָיְתָה

תֹהוּ וָבֹהוּ

והארץ , היתה תהו ובהו

והארץ , היתה תהו ובהו

Hebrew Writing 46

Today you are going to trace, write, and read the second part of Genesis 1:2. Remember to read and write from right to left! The part we are doing today is the underlined part of the Hebrew and the transliterated part that's big and bold. I know this is getting tricky. It's all foreign to you! Hang in there. Next year we'll start with the alphabet and writing and go further.

Genesis 1:2

וְהָאָרֶץ, הָיְתָה תֹהוּ וָבֹהוּ, וְחֹשֶׁךְ, עַל פְּנֵי תְהוֹם ; וְרוּחַ
אֱלֹהִים, מְרַחֶפֶת עַל פְּנֵי הַמָּיִם.

vehaArets haaTAH TOhu vaVOhu **veKHOshekh al pnaa teHOM ;**
veRUakh eloHEEM meraKHEfet al pnaa haMAyim

וחשך על פני
תהום ורוח

וחשך על פני תהום ורוח
וחשך על פני תהום ורוח

Hebrew Writing 47

Today you are going to trace, write, and read the last part of Genesis 1:2. Remember to read and write from right to left! The part we are doing today is the underlined part of the Hebrew and the transliterated part that's big and bold. With so many similar looking letters you can see why they say there were errors when copies of the Old Testament were handwritten.

Genesis 1:2

וְהָאָרֶץ, הָיְתָה תֹהוּ וָבֹהוּ, וְחֹשֶׁךְ, עַל פְּנֵי תְהוֹם ; וְרוּחַ אֱלֹהִים, מְרַחֶפֶת עַל פְּנֵי הַמָּיִם.

vehaArets haaTAH TOhu vaVOhu veKHOshekh al pnaa teHOM ; veRUakh

eloHEEM , meraKHEfet al pnaa haMAyim

אלהים מרחפת

על פני המים

אלהים מרחפת על

פני המים

Hebrew Writing 48

Genesis 1:1   be reSHEET baRA eloHEEM et ha shaMAyim ve et ha Arets

בְּרֵאשִׁית, בָּרָא אֱלֹהִים, אֵת הַשָּׁמַיִם, וְאֵת הָאָרֶץ.

Genesis 1:2
ve ha Arets haaTAH TOhu va VOhu ve KHOshekh al pnaa teHOM ve RUakh eloHEEM
meraKHEfet al pnaa ha MAyim

וְהָאָרֶץ, הָיְתָה תֹהוּ וָבֹהוּ, וְחֹשֶׁךְ, עַל פְּנֵי תְהוֹם ; וְרוּחַ
אֱלֹהִים, מְרַחֶפֶת עַל פְּנֵי הַמָּיִם.

Genesis 1:3
va YOmer eloHEEM yeHEE or va yeHEE or

וַיֹּאמֶר אֱלֹהִים, יְהִי אוֹר ; וַיְהִי אוֹר.

Hebrew Writing 49

Remember to work from right to left. Start with the Qof on the top right and trace that one first. Then move to the one to its left. When you get to the end of the row, go back to the bottom right and trace that letter.

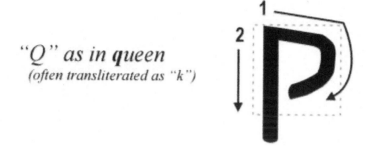

Trace Letter Qof!

"Q" as in queen
(often transliterated as "k")

Trace the letter outline:

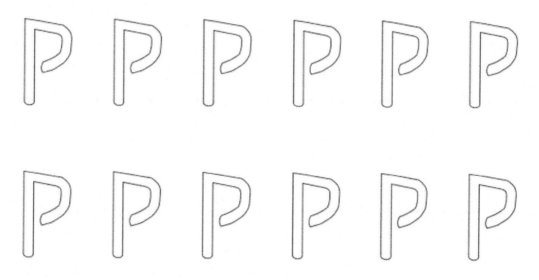

Can you find the Qof in Genesis 1:5?

וַיִּקְרָא אֱלֹהִים לָאוֹר יוֹם, וְלַחֹשֶׁךְ קָרָא לָיְלָה; וַיְהִי עֶרֶב וַיְהִי בֹקֶר, יוֹם אֶחָד.

There are two in this verse. Remember that different fonts look different!

Hebrew Writing 50

The first line is for calligraphy. Trace the second line of the letter Qof and then write your own. This is another letter that hangs down low. You can see it in Genesis 1:5 on the Hebrew Writing 49 page.

ק ק ק ק ק ק ק ק ק ק

ק ק ק ק ק ק ק ק ק ק

Hebrew Writing 51

Today you are going to trace, write, and read the first part of Genesis 1:5. Remember to read and write from right to left! The part we are doing today is the underlined part of the Hebrew and the transliterated part that's big and bold.

וַיִּקְרָא אֱלֹהִים לָאוֹר יוֹם, וְלַחֹשֶׁךְ קָרָא לָיְלָה; וַיְהִי עֶרֶב וַיְהִי בֹקֶר, יוֹם אֶחָד.

vayikRA eloHEEM laor yom velaKHOshekh kaRA LIl-la

va yeHEE Erev va yeHEE VOker yom ekHAD

ויקרא אלהים

לאור יום ולחשך

קרא לילה

ויקרא אלהים לאור יום ולחשך קרא לילה

Hebrew Writing 52

Today you are going to trace, write, and read the second part of Genesis 1:5. Remember to read and write from right to left! The part we are doing today is the underlined part of the Hebrew and the transliterated part that's big and bold.

וַיִּקְרָא אֱלֹהִים לָאוֹר יוֹם, וְלַחֹשֶׁךְ קָרָא לָיְלָה; וַיְהִי עֶרֶב וַיְהִי בֹקֶר, יוֹם אֶחָד.

va yikRA eloHEEM la or yom ve la KHOshekh kaRA LII-la **vayeHEE Erev**

vayeHEE VOker yom ekHAD

ויהי ערב ויהי בקר יום אחד

Hebrew Writing 53

Remember to work from right to left. Start with the Tet on the top right and trace that one first. Then move to the one to its left. When you get to the end of the row, go back to the bottom right and trace that letter.

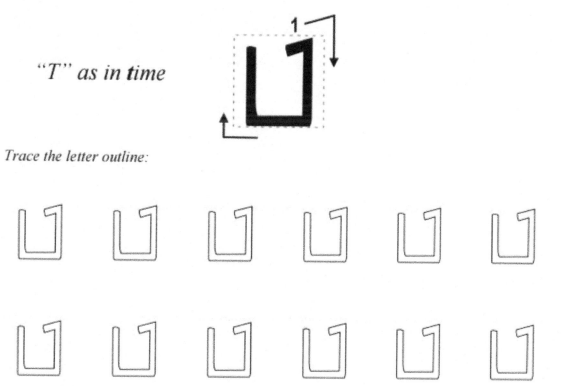

Trace Letter Tet!

"T" as in time

Trace the letter outline:

Can you find the Tet in Genesis 1:4?

וַיַּרְא אֱלֹהִים אֶת הָאוֹר, כִּי טוֹב; וַיַּבְדֵּל אֱלֹהִים, בֵּין הָאוֹר וּבֵין הַחֹשֶׁךְ.

Hebrew Writing 54

The first line is for calligraphy. Trace the second line of the letter Tet and then write your own. Then trace and write tov.

טוב

Hebrew Writing 55

The first line is for calligraphy. Trace the second line of the word ki and then write your own.

כִּי כִּי כִּי כִּי כִּי כִּי   **כִּי**

כִּי כִּי כִּי כִּי כִּי   **כִּי**

Hebrew Writing 56

Read and write Genesis 1:4.

va yar eloHEEM et ha or ki tov va yavDEL eloHEEM ben ha or u ven ha KHOshekh

vayar eloHEEM et haor, ki tov; vayavDEL eloHEEM, ben haor uven haKHOshekh

וַיַּרְא אֱלֹהִים אֶת הָאוֹר, כִּי טוֹב; וַיַּבְדֵּל אֱלֹהִים, בֵּין הָאוֹר וּבֵין הַחֹשֶׁךְ.

וירא אלהים את

האור כי טוב

ויבדל אלהים

בין האור ובין

החשך

Hebrew Writing 57

Genesis 1:1   be reSHEET baRA eloHEEM et ha shaMAyim ve et ha Arets

בְּרֵאשִׁית, בָּרָא אֱלֹהִים, אֵת הַשָּׁמַיִם, וְאֵת הָאָרֶץ.

Genesis 1:2
ve ha Arets haaTAH TOhu va VOhu ve KHOshekh al pnaa teHOM ve RUakh eloHEEM meraKHEfet al pnaa ha MAyim

וְהָאָרֶץ, הָיְתָה תֹהוּ וָבֹהוּ, וְחֹשֶׁךְ, עַל פְּנֵי תְהוֹם; וְרוּחַ אֱלֹהִים, מְרַחֶפֶת עַל פְּנֵי הַמָּיִם.

Genesis 1:3
va YOmer eloHEEM yeHEE or va yeHEE or

וַיֹּאמֶר אֱלֹהִים, יְהִי אוֹר; וַיְהִי אוֹר.

Genesis 1:4
va yar eloHEEM et ha or ki tov va yavDEL eloHEEM ben ha or u ven ha KHOshekh

וַיַּרְא אֱלֹהִים אֶת הָאוֹר, כִּי טוֹב; וַיַּבְדֵּל אֱלֹהִים, בֵּין הָאוֹר וּבֵין הַחֹשֶׁךְ.

Genesis 1:5
va yikRA eloHEEM la or yom ve la KHOshekh kaRA LII-la va yeHEE Erev va yehee VOker yom ekHAD

וַיִּקְרָא אֱלֹהִים לָאוֹר יוֹם, וְלַחֹשֶׁךְ קָרָא לָיְלָה; וַיְהִי עֶרֶב וַיְהִי בֹקֶר, יוֹם אֶחָד.

Now, turn the page and try to read it!

Genesis 1:1-5

א בְּרֵאשִׁית, בָּרָא אֱלֹהִים, אֵת הַשָּׁמַיִם, וְאֵת הָאָרֶץ.

ב וְהָאָרֶץ, הָיְתָה תֹהוּ וָבֹהוּ, וְחֹשֶׁךְ, עַל פְּנֵי תְהוֹם; וְרוּחַ אֱלֹהִים, מְרַחֶפֶת עַל פְּנֵי הַמָּיִם.

ג וַיֹּאמֶר אֱלֹהִים, יְהִי אוֹר; וַיְהִי אוֹר.

ד וַיַּרְא אֱלֹהִים אֶת הָאוֹר, כִּי טוֹב; וַיַּבְדֵּל אֱלֹהִים, בֵּין הָאוֹר וּבֵין הַחֹשֶׁךְ.

ה וַיִּקְרָא אֱלֹהִים לָאוֹר יוֹם, וְלַחֹשֶׁךְ קָרָא לָיְלָה; וַיְהִי עֶרֶב וַיְהִי בֹקֶר, יוֹם אֶחָד.

Appendix

100 Balloons for Understanding Percentages

The Periodic Table of Elements

1 H hydrogen 1.0079																	2 He helium 4.0026
3 Li lithium 6.941	4 Be beryllium 9.0122											5 B boron 10.811	6 C carbon 12.011	7 N nitrogen 14.007	8 O oxygen 15.999	9 F fluorine 18.998	10 Ne neon 20.180
11 Na sodium 22.990	12 Mg magnesium 24.305											13 Al aluminium 26.982	14 Si silicon 28.086	15 P phosphorus 30.974	16 S sulfur 32.065	17 Cl chlorine 35.453	18 Ar argon 39.948
19 K potassium 39.098	20 Ca calcium 40.078	21 Sc scandium 44.956	22 Ti titanium 47.867	23 V vanadium 50.942	24 Cr chromium 51.996	25 Mn manganese 54.938	26 Fe iron 55.845	27 Co cobalt 58.933	28 Ni nickel 58.693	29 Cu copper 63.546	30 Zn zinc 65.39	31 Ga gallium 69.723	32 Ge germanium 72.61	33 As arsenic 74.922	34 Se selenium 78.96	35 Br bromine 79.904	36 Kr krypton 83.80
37 Rb rubidium 85.468	38 Sr strontium 87.62	39 Y yttrium 88.906	40 Zr zirconium 91.224	41 Nb niobium 92.906	42 Mo molybdenum 95.94	43 Tc technetium [98]	44 Ru ruthenium 101.07	45 Rh rhodium 102.91	46 Pd palladium 106.42	47 Ag silver 107.87	48 Cd cadmium 112.41	49 In indium 114.82	50 Sn tin 118.71	51 Sb antimony 121.76	52 Te tellurium 127.60	53 I iodine 126.90	54 Xe xenon 131.29
55 Cs caesium 132.91	56 Ba barium 137.33	57-70 *	71 Lu lutetium 174.97	72 Hf hafnium 178.49	73 Ta tantalum 180.95	74 W tungsten 183.84	75 Re rhenium 186.21	76 Os osmium 190.23	77 Ir iridium 192.22	78 Pt platinum 195.08	79 Au gold 196.97	80 Hg mercury 200.59	81 Tl thallium 204.38	82 Pb lead 207.2	83 Bi bismuth 208.98	84 Po polonium [209]	85 At astatine [210]	86 Rn radon [222]
87 Fr francium [223]	88 Ra radium [226]	89-102 **	103 Lr lawrencium [262]	104 Rf rutherfordium [261]	105 Db dubnium [262]	106 Sg seaborgium [266]	107 Bh bohrium [264]	108 Hs hassium [269]	109 Mt meitnerium [268]	110 Uun ununnilium [271]	111 Uuu unununium [272]	112 Uub ununbium [277]	114 Uuq ununquadium [289]				

* Lanthanide series

57 La lanthanum 138.91	58 Ce cerium 140.12	59 Pr praseodymium 140.91	60 Nd neodymium 144.24	61 Pm promethium [145]	62 Sm samarium 150.36	63 Eu europium 151.96	64 Gd gadolinium 157.25	65 Tb terbium 158.93	66 Dy dysprosium 162.50	67 Ho holmium 164.93	68 Er erbium 167.26	69 Tm thulium 168.93	70 Yb ytterbium 173.04

** Actinide series

89 Ac actinium [227]	90 Th thorium 232.04	91 Pa protactinium 231.04	92 U uranium 238.03	93 Np neptunium [237]	94 Pu plutonium [244]	95 Am americium [243]	96 Cm curium [247]	97 Bk berkelium [247]	98 Cf californium [251]	99 Es einsteinium [252]	100 Fm fermium [257]	101 Md mendelevium [258]	102 No nobelium [259]

Day Number Index Some reviews are just part of the lesson and not in the workbook.

Day #

1, 2	Writing Sentences 1
6	Writing Sentences 2
11	Writing Sentences 3
16	Writing Sentences 4
21	Writing Sentences 5
36	Writing Sentences 6
41	Writing Sentences 7
46	Writing Sentences 8
51	Writing Sentences 9
56	Writing Sentences 10
71	Writing Sentences 11
76	Writing Sentences 12
81	Writing Sentences 13
86	Writing Sentences 14
91	Writing Sentences 15
106	Writing Sentences 16
111	Writing Sentences 17
116	Writing Sentences 18
121	Writing Sentences 19
126	Writing Sentences 20

26	Spelling Review 1
27	Spelling Review 2
28	Spelling Review 3
29	Spelling Review 4
30	Spelling Review 5
61	Spelling Review 6
62	Spelling Review 7
63	Spelling Review 8
64	Spelling Review 9
65	Spelling Review 10
96	Spelling Review 11
97	Spelling Review 12
98	Spelling Review 13
99	Spelling Review 14
100	Spelling Review 15
131	Spelling Review 16
132	Spelling Review 17
133	Spelling Review 18
134	Spelling Review 19
135	Spelling Review 20

Day #

31	Grammar Review 1
33	Grammar Review 2
35	Grammar Review 3
67	Grammar Review 4
69	Grammar Review 5
101	Grammar Review 6
103	Grammar Review 7
105	Grammar Review 8
136	Grammar Review 9
140	Grammar Review 10

32	Vocabulary Review 1
34	Vocabulary Review 2
66	Vocabulary Review 3
68	Vocabulary Review 4
70	Vocabulary Review 5
102	Vocabulary Review 6
104	Vocabulary Review 7
137	Vocabulary Review 8
139	Vocabulary Review 9

27	Science Review 2
32	Science Review 4
33	Science Review 5
64	Science Review 9
65	Science Review 10
75	Science Review 11
90	Science Review 12
97	Science Review 13
99	Science Review 14
100	Science Review 15
106	Science Review 16
131, 136	Science Review 17
134	Science Review 18

Day #	
29	Social Studies 2
35	Social Studies 4
47	Social Studies 5
67	Social Studies 7
68	Social Studies 8
69	Social Studies 9
70	Social Studies 10
90	Social Studies 11
101, 102	Social Studies 12
131-140	Social Studies 14
136	Social Studies 15
137	Social Studies 16
138	Social Studies 17
140	Social Studies 18
141-145	Social Studies 19
72, 73	Hebrew Writing 1
74, 75	Hebrew Writing 2
77, 78	Hebrew Writing 3
79, 80	Hebrew Writing 4
82, 83	Hebrew Writing 5
84	Hebrew Writing 6
85	Hebrew Writing 7
87, 88	Hebrew Writing 8
89	Hebrew Writing 9
90	Hebrew Writing 10
92, 93	Hebrew Writing 11
94	Hebrew Writing 12
95	Hebrew Writing 13
97, 98	Hebrew Writing 14
99	Hebrew Writing 15
100	Hebrew Writing 16
102, 103	Hebrew Writing 17
104	Hebrew Writing 18
105	Hebrew Writing 19
106	Hebrew Writing 20
107	Hebrew Writing 21
108	Hebrew Writing 22
109	Hebrew Writing 23
110	Hebrew Writing 24
111	Hebrew Writing 25
112	Hebrew Writing 26
113	Hebrew Writing 27

Day #	
114	Hebrew Writing 28
115	Hebrew Writing 29
116	Hebrew Writing 30
117	Hebrew Writing 31
118	Hebrew Writing 32
119	Hebrew Writing 33
120	Hebrew Writing 34
122	Hebrew Writing 35
124	Hebrew Writing 36
125	Hebrew Writing 37
126	Hebrew Writing 38
127	Hebrew Writing 39
128	Hebrew Writing 40
129	Hebrew Writing 41
130	Hebrew Writing 42
131	Hebrew Writing 43
132	Hebrew Writing 44
133	Hebrew Writing 45
134	Hebrew Writing 46
135	Hebrew Writing 47
136	Hebrew Writing 48
137	Hebrew Writing 49
138	Hebrew Writing 50
139	Hebrew Writing 51
140	Hebrew Writing 52
142	Hebrew Writing 53
143	Hebrew Writing 54
144	Hebrew Writing 55
145	Hebrew Writing 56
146-	Hebrew Writing 57

Thank you for using

Genesis Curriculum
The Book of Genesis

We hope you had a great year learning together.

Genesis Curriculum also offers:

GC Steps: This is GC's preschool and kindergarten curriculum. There are three years (ages three through six) where kids will learn to read and write as well as develop beginning math skills.

A Mind for Math: This is GC's elementary school learning-together math program based on the curriculum's daily Bible reading. Children work together as well as have their own leveled workbook.

Rainbow Readers: These are leveled reading books. They each have a unique dictionary with the included words underlined in the text. They are also updated to use modern American spelling.

Look for more years of the Genesis Curriculum using both Old and New Testament books of the Bible. Find us online to read about the latest developments in this expanding curriculum.

GenesisCurriculum.com

44585265R00119

Made in the USA
Middletown, DE
08 May 2019